MADE IN SCOTLAND

CAROL FOREMAN

BIRLINN

This edition first published in 2019 by
Birlinn Limited West Newington House
10 Newington Road Edinburgh EH9 1QS
www.birlinn.co.uk

Originally published in 2004 by Birlinn Ltd

Images reproduced courtesy of
Robert Opie, pages 10/17/20/22/26/46/51/78/79/88/89/107/108
Historyworld, page 75

ISBN 978 1 78027 6090

British Library Cataloguing-in-Publication Data A catalogue record for this book is
available from the British Library

Typeset in Gill Sans
Design: seagulls.net
Printed and bound in China

INTRODUCTION

Of the wide range and diversity of British products in the marketplace, both at home and abroad, the Scots can take pride in the fact that many of them began in Scotland and are now household names.

For example, Dr E. J. Mills, a chemist at the Royal Technical College, Glasgow, invented that well-known bleach Parozone in 1891. When people around the world spread Robertson's 'Golden Shred' marmalade on their toast, it is courtesy of Paisley man James Robertson and his wife, Marion. How would cooks thicken their sauces easily without cornflour, first produced in Paisley by Brown & Polson in 1854?

The world's first concentrated bottled fruit drink was Rose's Lime Juice Cordial, invented by Leith man Lachlan Rose. The finest shortbread in the world is produced by Walkers of Aberlour, and the UK's No. 1 comic, *The Beano*, is published in Dundee.

The world's best-selling Scotch whisky is Johnnie Walker Red Label, bottled in Kilmarnock. Glenfiddich Distillery in Dufftown produces the world's best-selling malt whisky.

Dewar & Sons' Aberfeldy Distillery produces the biggest selling scotch whisky in the US. Scotland's 'Other National Drink', Irn-Bru, is an international brand that began in the Gallowgate in Glasgow in 1901. On the bottled water front, Highland Spring in Perthshire is the UK's No. 1 sparkling water brand.

Pringle of Hawick gave the world the knitted twin-set, and J & P Coats of Paisley, whose origins go back to 1830, grew to become the largest thread manufacturer in the world. In the bathroom, the Shanks part of the internationally known Armitage Shanks refers to John Shanks of Paisley.

Made in Scotland features the stories behind forty household names that began in Scotland, most of which have stood the test of time. Some that have not, however, such as British Caledonian Airways and Templeton Carpets, are fondly remembered and appear in the section entitled 'Gone, But Not Forgotten'.

Many of the stories behind the contributions to daily life given to us by Scots are fascinating, as they are those of enterprising young people who achieved their aims, not by plentiful funds but through the Scottish virtues of hard work, perseverance, integrity, courage and initiative. While they all began their business lives in a small way or by chance, against all the odds they were successful, like William Younger, who laid the foundations of what became the brewery giant Scottish & Newcastle, now named Heineken UK. Among Scottish institutions, The Royal Bank of Scotland, established in 1727, grew into the fifth largest bank in the world.

While, sadly, some of the brands featured in *Made in Scotland* have been taken over by multi- national companies and are no longer manufactured in Scotland, others are still being manufactured in the land of their birth. Some are even owned, or are being managed by, descendants of the founders.

Apart from being a compilation of famous brands that began in Scotland and a salute to Scottish industry and the remarkable people who made it great, *Made in Scotland* is a nostalgic journey into the past.

CONTENTS

Design

Shanks
sanitary appliances

HEAD OFFICE : SHANKS & CO., LTD., TUBAL WORKS, BARRHEAD SCOTLAND
Also at, London, Manchester, Newcastle-on-Tyne, Glasgow, Bristol, Belfast

Glamorous 1940s
Ideal Home *magazine*
advertisement.

01

Armitage Shanks

The name 'Armitage Shanks' is ubiquitous in the world of bathrooms, and millions of people use one of its products every day.

The company came about when two long established companies, one named after a place and the other after a person, amalgamated. The place is Armitage in Staffordshire and the person is John Shanks. For our purposes, it is the Shanks part of the Armitage Shanks' story that we are interested in.

John Shanks was born in Paisley in 1825, and was the son of a handloom weaver. He was apprenticed as a plumber to Wallace and Connell of Glasgow, going on to work as a journeyman plumber in the Paisley area until, aged 30, he started his own plumbing business in Barrhead, eight miles from Glasgow.

Being an innovative man, John Shanks began to devise improvements to sanitary ware, and in 1863 his first patent was for a trapless water closet, the 'Patent Flexible Valve Closet'. Nationwide sales of the product, known simply in the product catalogue as 'Number Four', brought success to the company. In 1875, John and his brother Andrew, also a plumber, founded Shanks and Co. Sanitary Engineers. Around this time, to manufacture the fittings for John's various inventions, the company also opened a small

Top left. A John Shanks' patent of 1892 – his 'modern' bath.

Above: Shanks' Siphonic Closet advertised in 1896 in The Bailie Magazine.

brass foundry that would become the famous Tubal Works.

In 1877, John took out a patent for delivering water to basins through side inlets. A similar design was used in the 1880s on the company's Citizen washbasins and Imperial baths. Only the spindle and knobs of the tap were exposed, and the water entered the basin through small perforations in the earthenware. Basins were sometimes fitted with innovative hair-washing apparatus.

In 1884, Shanks exhibited the 'Eureka' canopy bath at the International Health Exhibition in South Kensington. It was fitted with a full range of shower effects and was enclosed in an elegant wooden cabinet. The 'Eureka' was described as 'the acme of luxurious bathing'. By the mid-1880s, Shanks advertised their 'Patent Pedestal Bidet', with hot and cold water and

an ascending spray, claiming it was 'a very necessary appliance in a well-appointed bathroom'. This continental appliance, however, was little-understood and even mistrusted in Britain and America.

By the 1890s the firm occupied a seven-acre site and employed 600 men. By 1894 John had taken out around 100 patents, and the company had established itself as Britain's leader in sanitary engineering.

John Shanks died in December 1895, after which his son John and his nephew William carried on the business. John always looked after his employees, providing in his will an extra day's pay to those who had been with the company for six months on the day of his death.

After John's death the company continued to flourish, and around 1900 the Victoria Pottery was established to ensure uniformity of quality and economy in production.

At the same time a showroom was opened at 81 Bond Street, London to allow for a larger share of the West End trade. Shanks' business was not confined to Britain, though; it exported tens of thousands of products overseas, ensuring an international reputation.

The firm was run by the Shanks family until 1969, when it merged with Armitage Ware to form Armitage Shanks. The Armitage part of the business was founded in 1817 by Thomas Bond in Armitage, Staffordshire. In 1980, Armitage Shanks became a member of the Blue Circle Industries Group. In 1992 the Barrhead factory closed, and today, Armitage Shanks is a brand of Ideal Standard International Brands.

armitage shanks Ⓐ
All the best in your bathroom

A Bathroom Revisited

Relive those days of traditional Victorian splendour with the exclusive Dolphin Bathroom by Armitage Shanks.

Period authenticity features throughout. Real mahogany, hand decorated vitreous china, real polished brass fittings, even decorative wall brackets.

Armitage Shanks' advertisement c.1984 advertising the exclusive Dolphin range that revives the days of traditional Victorian splendour.

Left: Label for Ethel Baxter's famous Royal Game Soup.

Below: Label from an early product, Little Scarlet Strawberry Jam.

02

The Scots are the biggest consumers of soup in Europe, and if there's a company that's famous for the quality of its soups it's Baxters Food Group.

The beginnings of the world-renowned food manufacturing company were firmly embedded in the Highlands of Scotland. It was founded by George Baxter, originally one of fifty or so gardeners employed by the Duke of Richmond on his estate at Castle Gordon, near Fochabers, on the banks of the River Spey.

George then decided that gardening was not for him, and with the backing of his wife, Margaret, the Duke's blessing and a £100 loan from various family members, he opened a little grocery shop in Spey Street, Fochabers, in 1868.

With the Scottish virtues of hard work, integrity and initiative behind it, the business prospered. George served in the front of the shop while in the back Margaret made jams and jellies, mainly from fruit gathered in the grounds of nearby Castle Gordon. Apart from the locals, their customers included members of shooting and fishing parties and the Duke of Gordon's guests, who, after buying and enjoying Margaret's jams and jellies, left orders to be delivered to their home addresses.

There was more however to the Baxter shop than groceries and jams. George Baxter was also a whisky

A 1980's tin can wrap design featuring all the enduring Baxters brand elements trading on its Scottishness and, in this case, containing a very Scottish dish.

wholesaler. He bought malt whisky from local distilleries, bottled it and sold it under the trade name of Baxter's Pure Malt Scotch Whisky. George also travelled to London and Europe for the fine cheeses, pâtés and wines required by the gentry and the Duke of Gordon, to whose castle he delivered a daily order.

As he grew up, George and Margaret's son William developed a love for the business, and at thirteen, he left school and joined his father full-time. At an early age, he had shown considerable ability as a salesman, and by the time he was eighteen he was accompanying his father on buying visits to London and Europe while his younger brother, George, looked after the shop. His selling trips, however, were not always congenial. His northern route would begin by taking his bicycle by train to Wick and then, in all weathers, cycling all the way back to Fochabers, handing out samples and taking orders as he went. It was William's wife, Ethel, who in 1914 decided that, as sales of jams were so good, she and William should leave the family grocery shop to William's brother, George, and set up on their own as jam manufacturers. To this end, William approached the family's patron, the Duke of Gordon, and after Church one Sunday, the Duke and William marked out with wooden pegs and pieces of string a suitable site for a jam factory one mile from Fochabers on the other side of the Spey River. Since then, the factory has

been extended many times but is still located at the same beautiful site.

William ventured beyond the Border in the 1920s. With letters of introduction from the Duke of Gordon, he went to London and obtained orders from such famous companies as Harrods, Fortnum & Mason and the Army and Navy Stores. He even received orders from Buckingham Palace. When he gave his sales pitch to the buyer of Fortnum & Mason, the buyer said with a smile that he could not understand a word of it. Ethel's preserves, however, spoke for themselves and William still got his order.

In 1929, taking advantage of the ready supply of venison, beef and game in her part of Scotland, the inventive Ethel created and canned the now world-famous Royal Game Soup. She then went on to pioneer soft fruit canning in Scotland and to produce jars of beetroot, canned haggis and more delicious jams and marmalade.

By the end of the 1930s, Baxters was known for its quality products, but, in common with other businesses, it was hard hit by the Second World War. The rebuilding of the business was put into the hands of William and Ethel's sons Gordon and Ian. With Gordon covering Scotland as a one-man sales force, as his father had done many years before, and Ian in charge of production, gradually things began to move again despite money being scarce and raw materials being allocated by the government. The brothers had to beg for can allocations from the Metal Box Company, and they searched everywhere to source used-glass jars for their jams. They were determined to build the business, however, and to base it on quality products such as Ethel's Royal Game Soup and her beetroot products.

Like Baxter wives before her, Gordon's wife, Ena, an artist, became an important factor in the company's development. She had seen a recipe for a Louisiana chicken gumbo soup in the American magazine *Gourmet,* and decided to make it to find out what it was like. However, as it contained an unusual vegetable called okra, an unobtainable green pepper found in the southern states of America, she substituted green beans from her garden. The result was a soup about which her husband was so enthusiastic that he wanted to can it immediately. Ena, however, insisted it should be perfected first.

Despite warnings of commercial disaster from well-meaning customers who thought it would be impossible to compete with the giant companies that controlled the British soup market, in 1953 Gordon and Ena introduced a range of Scottish soups, and by the third year had sold a million cans. It was an exciting period in the history of the company and the beginning of its post-war growth – 'a Highland romance' as one journalist called it.

Later came exciting varieties such as Cock-a-leekie, Lobster Bisque, Pheasant Consommé, and Cream of Smoked Trout, all made from local ingredients. Sauces, chutneys, canned game birds and a wide range of traditional Scottish foodstuffs were also produced to Ena's recipes.

Ena Baxter tested all new products in her kitchen at home, and if her family liked them, they were taken to the experimental kitchen at the factory where they were tried out. A cosy family image sold the product, and advertisements showed Ena Baxter chopping and stirring ingredients for soups and sauces to feed her family. The message was that if it was good enough for the Baxter family, it was good enough for the Baxter brand.

Baxters began to export worldwide and when trying to sell his products in America in the 1950s, Gordon Baxter learned that it's not sufficient to try to sell what you make. First, you had to find out what the customer wanted, make it and then advertise it. His discovery changed his business, and he and Ena turned it upside down.

Despite around 182 takeover approaches, the company remains private and is today run by the fourth generation of the Baxter family. Gordon's daughter, Audrey, is the chairman, and she puts the company's continuing success quite simply down to passion and innovation: 'We are passionate at Baxters about good food, which means finding the finest ingredients and creating innovative recipes that are right for today's highly discerning consumers throughout the world.' Still a very independent family firm, Baxters faces the future with pride and a determination to stay ahead.

Ena and George Baxter. Ena joined the family company in 1952 and was a very talented cook. The launch of her range of soups was a turning point in the company's history.

11

The cover of The Beano's *65th birthday edition shows, as well as Dennis the Menace, characters from the past such as Big Eggo, Tin Can Tommy, Pin the Elastic Man, Tom Thumb, Big Fat Joe, Whoopee Hank and Morgan the Mighty.*

03

THE BEANO

You could be forgiven for thinking that, in today's technology-driven world, children would find a comic such as *The Beano*, which is largely unchanged since the 1950s, somewhat dated and boring.

You would be wrong, as *The Beano* is the UK's No. 1 comic, with a weekly circulation of over 37,000. Children love its propaganda-free, timeless humour, stemming from the activities of mischievous characters such as Dennis the Menace, Minnie the Minx, Roger the Dodger and the Bash Street Kids, who flout authority and cause mayhem.

Following on the success of *The Dandy*, introduced on 4 December 1937, Dundee publisher D. C. Thomson launched a sister comic, *The Beano*, on 30 July 1938. It

cost 2d (less than one pence) at which price it remained until 1960. Very few copies of the early *Beanos* exist, and a copy of *Beano* No. 1 was sold for £12,000 in 2004. Not a bad return for 2d.

The Dandy and *Beano* created fantasy worlds in which children could question the probability of their exploits, but not the standards of their behaviour or attitudes. There was a moral code. Parental and school authority might be challenged, but there was inevitably a punishment to suit the crime. The humour was

basic, with the fun emanating from a wide selection of cartoon characters that readers could relate to, sympathise with and laugh at in ridiculous incidents and

The Beano's first cover, introducing Big Eggo, the ostrich who ate everything in sight.

situations, set against the social conditions of the time. Pure slapstick was avoided.

Today the comics' editors are ever conscious of the unique hold their characters have on their readers, and while the humour is unchanged, with maturity came responsibility – such as when the Home Office asked that care be taken when using fireworks in stories. Now November 5 is not marked at all. Corporal punishment was banned, not because of any concern that psychologists expressed on the so-called violence of comic strips, but because the editors agreed that the social conditions of the time must be reflected.

The format of *The Beano* was similar to that of *The Dandy*: twenty-eight pages with a mix of short, funny strips, adventure picture stories and text stories. Among the adventure stories was the tiniest character in comic history, Tom Thumb. There was also the Shipwrecked Circus and Jimmy and His Magic Patch. In the latter, Jimmy Watson had a patch made from a piece of magic carpet sewn on to the seat of his trousers and, by simply wishing out loud, he was whisked back in time to have adventures with historical and legendary characters such as Sinbad the Sailor, William Tell and Ali Baba. All these stories were drawn by Dudley Dexter Watkins, whose genius created some of the finest cartoon characters in history and to whom much of the early success of *The Dandy* and *Beano* can be attributed.

Soon after the launch of *The Beano* came the Second World War, and, although shortage of paper meant that *The Beano* and *Dandy*

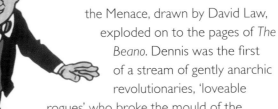

were reduced to twelve pages per issue and published fortnightly (on alternate weeks), it was felt that to continue publishing the comics would help keep up the morale of the nation's children.

Although the comics were non-political in peacetime, the war years saw an element of propaganda in support of the British war effort. Two liquorice black eyes were given as a gift in 1940, which was to be the last gift for over twenty years.

Publication restrictions continued after the war, and by 1947 the comics were down to ten pages, which was increased to twelve in 1948 at which figure they remained until 1960 when they were increased to sixteen pages. In 1971, they went up to twenty pages. Weekly publication was resumed in 1949, and a year later the word 'comic' was dropped from the titles.

When the wartime restrictions were finally over, the comics gradually returned to normal, with *The Dandy* narrowly the top seller. Then, on 17 March 1951, Dennis

the Menace, drawn by David Law, exploded on to the pages of *The Beano*. Dennis was the first of a stream of gently anarchic revolutionaries, 'loveable rogues' who broke the mould of the fantasy-based characters that had populated *The Beano* until then.

Dennis's first words were: 'Keep off the grass. huh!' In 1968, Dennis's faithful sidekick, Gnasher, an extremely rare Abyssinian wire-haired tripe hound, joined in the mayhem. Gnasher was modelled on Dennis's black hair, to which were added eyes, nose, legs and teeth that could bite through granite. Dennis made the cover in 1974, and two years later the Dennis the Menace Fan Club (including Gnasher's Fang Club) was formed.

The second of the new breed of characters was Roger the Dodger, who began ducking, dodging and diving on 18 April 1953. Drawn by Ken Reid, Roger earned his title, 'the craftiest schoolboy on earth', by using his endless collection of 'dodge' books to avoid doing any work. After Roger came Minnie the Minx, who made life a misery for her mum and dad and anyone else who dared to cross her path since she appeared on 19 December 1953 with the words: 'Yes, ma dear!' (quickly followed by) 'Oo-woo-woo! I'm on the warpath! take that, Charlie!' Dressed like her male counterpart and hero, Dennis the Menace, in a red and black hooped jersey,

her famous red pom-pomed beret, which doubles as a deadly Frisbee, hid her red hair, proving that red means danger.

The last of the revolutionaries was a gang whose members arrived on 13 February 1954. The strip, consisting of three introductory pictures and one large frame of a chaotic scene, began as 'When the Bell Rings' with the words: 'Hi, sleepy! Open the door – it's four.' Two years later, the gang became the Bash Street Kids, who struck terror into the heart of their teacher. Although the Bash Street Kids usually got the better of their teacher, in the end authority almost always asserted itself.

The idea for the Bash Street Kids came to *The Beano*'s first editor, George Moonie, as he looked out of his window, which faced the playground of Dundee's High School. As he watched the children play there was mayhem, and he realised that this was what he wanted for a strip. George commissioned Leo Baxendale to draw it, and *The Beano*'s readership so loved the antics of the nine rascals who became the Bash Street Kids, that by 1962 only Dennis the Menace was more popular.

Episodes of the Bash Street Kids no longer end with the teacher setting about the children with his cane. Punishments such as clamping their skateboards are used instead, and although the Kids are still dressed as 1950s' children in shorts, jumpers,

The strip, created by Leo Baxendale as When the Bell Rings, *first appeared in issue 604. It became* The Bash Street Kids *in 1956 and has become a regular feature, appearing in every issue.*

THE BASH STREET KIDS

caps and lace-up shoes rather than jeans and trainers, they now have mobile phones and play computer games. Their speech has also been updated. They used to speak the Queen's English with proper grammar, the only slang being the occasional 'Cripes'. Now they use Americanised slang, such as the sarcastic 'Not!'

While the heart of *The Beano* is still rooted in the stars introduced in the 1950s, the characters remain fresh by reacting to the modern world – Roger the Dodger can store his best dodges on a hard disk and the most enduring character, Dennis the Menace, has traded his cartie for a futuristic, gadget-filled Menace car. Dennis and Co. can also be found in jigsaws, as figurines, on spectacles, motorcycle helmets and cake-mix packs, to name but a few.

In 1998, *The Beano* Club was launched, signing up 50,000 members in its first year. Every member, including personality honorary members like Sean Connery, Princes Harry and William, Stephen Hendry and Michael Owen, received their T-shirt, poster, practical jokes and other goodies, plus regular deliveries of newsletters and birthday cards.

Many characters have come and gone in *The Beano*'s lifetime. Most traits, habits, attributes and characteristics have been exploited and are still being exploited – nosiness, greed, cowardice, absent-mindedness, mischief-making, sneakiness, courage, strength and exceptional skills. When characters no longer appeal, updated ones take their place.

That the old-age pensioner *Beano*, with its style largely unchanged since the 1950s, is Britain's favourite comic proves that children still love good old-fashioned knockabout fun, especially when it knocks authority. The comic has never lost touch with its readers and will surely continue to delight generations to come with fun-loving characters that will embrace new trends and technology as the years go by.

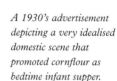

04

A 1930's advertisement depicting a very idealised domestic scene that promoted cornflour as bedtime infant supper.

Cornflour, used by cooks worldwide to thicken soups, sauces and gravies, was first produced in Paisley by Brown & Polson.

The history of the company began in 1840 when two muslin manufacturers, William Brown & Son and John Polson & Co., formed a joint enterprise to find a starch to bleach the muslin they produced. (The firm of William Brown had recently located to Paisley from Glasgow.) The joint enterprise, comprising a partner from each firm, William Brown and John Polson Snr, set up a bleaching, scouring and starching works at Thrushcraigs, near Paisley.

While researching for the most suitable starch for the two companies' finished muslin goods, John Polson discovered that a mixture of sago and flour made an ideal starch that could withstand bleaching. The idea then occurred to him that the starch might be suitable for household use, and in 1842 he introduced 'Powder Starch', which was first sold in Edinburgh in packages costing a penny and upwards. The name 'Powder Starch' came about as, for the first time, the starch was

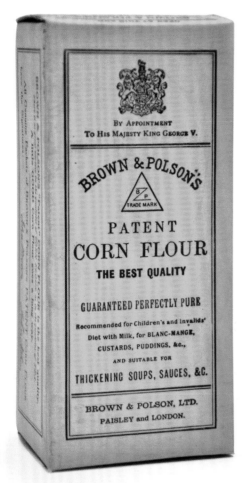

Early Packaging for Brown & Polson's Patent Corn Flour.

not in the form of 'pipes' or 'crystals' resembling basaltic column in miniature, the only form in which it had previously been known.

Because it was the only starch available to the domestic market, Powder Starch was a huge success and was awarded a certificate of merit at the Great Exhibition of 1851.

John Polson Senior died in 1843 at just forty-three years old, only a year after the introduction of Powder Starch. After his death, the firms of William Brown & Son and John Polson & Co. were amalgamated as Brown & Polson (Royal Starch Works).

The greatest breakthrough in the history of Brown & Polson came from John Polson Jnr, who discovered that if the fatty content was extracted from maize (also known as Indian corn), the substance remaining was a palatable pure starch. John then took out a patent in 1854 to market it as a foodstuff and soon the first packets of 'Brown & Polson's Patent Corn Flour' were in the shops. The new product, used as a basis for blancmanges, custards, baby and invalid foods, and as a thickener for soups and gravies, made the company world famous. Later the name was changed to 'cornflour' without capital letters.

As the firm prospered, new buildings were required and the original works at Thrushcraigs were supplemented by others at Barterholm and Colinslee. Eventually, all sites were concentrated at Carriagehill, Paisley, and then at splendid new works in the town's Falside Road. These new works were described in 1881, in a 'Treatise on the manufacture

of Starch, etc.' by Robert Hutter of Philadelphia, as among 'the most gigantic establishments of the kind'. The business continued to grow, and by 1896 it was described thus: 'Suppose that all the bags of Indian corn crushed at these works in one year were piled on top of each other, they would form a column 80 miles high.' In Paisley, Brown & Polson workers were always recognisable, as they were usually covered in a white coating of flour.

John Polson was deeply concerned about the welfare of his workers, and in the 1870s he introduced a profit-sharing scheme in the form of a yearly bonus based on the firm's profits. The bonus was paid to workers provided they were not 'guilty of misdemeanour', and to teach them a lesson in thrift, the bonus was paid directly to their credit in the local savings bank.

By the turn of the century Brown & Polson had become the largest manufacturer of starch products in Britain. Its best-known products were Patent Cornflour, Paisley Flour, Raisley Flour (self- raising), Blancmange, and Custard Powder. Later the company produced Mazola cooking oil as a by-product of maize. (It is interesting to note that over the years the by-products of maize were incorporated into the making of not only margarine and paper, but into the life-saving medicines of streptomycin and penicillin.)

Following the death of John Polson in 1900, the business was continued by J. Armour Brown and his three sons who were later joined by Lord Rowallan, connected by marriage to the Polson family.

Although by the start of the 1930s Brown & Polson was still the largest starch manufacturing company in the UK, the plant was old and new capital was required. To this end, in 1935 Brown & Polson became a wholly-owned subsidiary of Corn Products Company Ltd, an affiliate company of the American

Corn Products Refining Company, which had a manufacturing site in Manchester.

Throughout the years, the original firm published cookery books promoting the use of cornflour and custard powder. One was called *Light Fare Recipes for Corn Flour and 'Raisley' Cookery*, and as well as containing recipes for culinary delights such as 'Paisley Rolls' and 'Paisley Diamonds', it had price lists of cooking utensils and illustrations of them. Of course, the recipes insisted that the best ingredients the housewife could use were Brown & Polson's own products, 'Raisley' or 'Paisley Corn Flour'.

While the Royal Starch Works at Paisley were enlarged in 1950, in 1964 all starch manufacturing was transferred to Manchester. In 1962, however, the factory became the home of Knorr, making soups, stock cubes and sauces. Two years later, the manufacture of baby foods was introduced, in conjunction with the Gerber Company of America.

Among other brands introduced to Paisley by its parent company were Frank Cooper's Marmalade and Preserves and Hellman's Mayonnaise. Further products were adhesives, derived from starch, and dextrosol glucose powder and tablets. The company was still a leading manufacturer of cornflour, custard powder and blancmanges.

The most tragic event in the history of Brown & Polson occurred at 6.40am on 5 June 1964 when an explosion destroyed the animal feed plant. Workers arriving for their shift at 6.45am had to flee for their lives,

and as firemen, ambulance men and workers searched the rubble for casualties, people waited fearfully for news of their loved ones. Four men were killed and four were badly injured. A policeman at the scene commented: 'I have seen terrible things during the war, but never anything like this.'

Despite having such a wide range of products, from the 1970s the Paisley workforce was hit by major redundancies, with threats of closure if they were not accepted. These, however, were only stays of execution, and in 1996, the factory, which had employed so many Paisley men and women throughout its long life, was demolished.

Today Brown & Polson cornflour is manufactured by Knighton Foods in Adbaston, Staffordshire under licence to Premier Foods.

A 1938 advertisement for Brown & Polson's Corn Flour.

MY GRAVY IS TWICE AS TASTY AND FAR LESS TROUBLE TO MAKE NOW I THICKEN WITH BROWN & POLSON CORN FLOUR. NO LUMPS! NO HARD STIRRING! THE GRAVY COMES SMOOTH RIGHT AWAY!

BROWN & POLSON CORN FLOUR

An advertisement from the late 1890s when Camp Coffee was regular issue to all British soldiers where ever they were serving in the world.

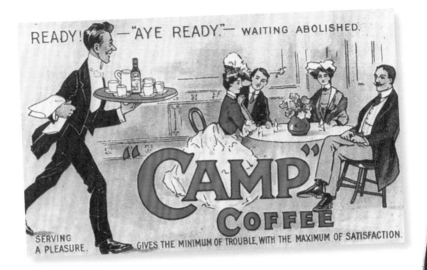

05

In 1885 in Glasgow, R. Paterson & Sons launched a product that became a worldwide household name – 'Camp' liquid coffee and chicory essence.

Its distinctive taste and instant readiness for use whenever wanted, with no loss of time waiting until beans were ground, accounted for its popularity. A single cup, or a gallon, could be produced at a moment's notice, and whether made by the cook, the lady of the house or her youngest daughter, the quality was always the same.

Apparently, the name 'Camp' derived from that of its originator, Campbell Paterson, son of Robert Paterson, who had started a small vinegar and pickle business in Hutcheson Street, Glasgow, in 1849. Campbell joined the company in 1868 and began to market their traditional product under the name of 'Paterson's Golden Grain Vinegar'. He also introduced

cordials and fruit wines to the range. Raspberry vinegar was a speciality and was made to meet the demand for raspberry flavourings in the spirit shops, where it was mixed with whisky to produce a drink favourable to the female palate and popularly called 'Cuddle-me-Dearie'. However, Campbell Paterson's most important contribution was introducing coffee essence to the company's beverage range.

The market for a commercial coffee product came when the drying, roasting, grinding and subsequent extraction of a coffee-flavoured essence was pioneered by several firms in Edinburgh, and in Glasgow by Robert Paterson & Son. Previously, domestic coffee drinking was a luxury enjoyed only by the affluent.

Top left: Ready Aye Ready – waiting abolished. Postcard c.1905 that plays on the product's instant readiness for use whenever wanted, with no loss of time waiting until beans were ground.

Above: The connection between the military and colonial Britain that was used so successfully in all their early marketing was the linchpin of the Patterson's domination of the coffee essence market.

Scotland became the major centre for the manufacture of coffee essence, capturing about 80 per cent of the market. Camp, however, was the market leader, its prominence mainly due to its superior quality but also to dynamic marketing techniques, innovative advertising and Campbell Paterson's far-sightedness in taking out a patent and trademark – a red seal with the words 'Camp Coffee' – to protect his company's special process. Even his workers were sworn to secrecy. Several types of coffee were blended in making Camp, with chicory added to give greater flavour and extra strength.

From the earliest days, Camp has been associated with a colonial military image, as the product's distinctive, tall square bottle's label depicts an Indian sepoy serving a cup of Camp to a kilted British officer outside his tent in some far outpost of the Empire. It is thought that the model for the officer was Sir Hector MacDonald, a general in the Boer War. Only his head was used, however. The uniform was deliberately drawn to avoid representing that of any particular regiment. It was also thought that depicting a general might provoke ill-feeling and possibly action by the War Office. In 1954, when the company tried to register the 'Highlander' alone as a trademark, the War Office would not allow a soldier in uniform to be used in such a way. A few years later, the registration was accepted. The motto on the label – 'Ready Aye Ready' – is not traceable to any particular family, but was used as a battle cry by several clans.

By 1898, Paterson was exporting coffee essence to all Britain's dependencies, and as every soldier in Queen Victoria's army throughout the Empire had a bottle of Camp tucked away in his kitbag, it was just as likely to be drunk around a campfire in the Khyber Pass as in a Glasgow drawing room. The Canadian, Australian and New Zealand markets were especially strong, but stringent tariffs according to value on both essence and bottles kept Paterson's from expanding into the lucrative American market.

While the prominent position of Camp was undoubtedly due to the excellence of the product, it was backed up by some of the most effective advertising of the day, earning Paterson's product international acclaim and recognition. Advertisements were always eye-catching, highly creative and artistic.

Paterson was the leading coffee essence producer in the Empire, and although there were well over one hundred producers of coffee essence or extract in Britain, the sales of Camp equalled the total sales of *all* the other producers.

In the post-war period the marketing campaigns acquired a far more domestic focus as this advertisement from the 1950s illustrates.

06

The story of Coats, the world leader in thread, began with James Coats, the son of George Coats who, in around 1760, moved from Dykehead to Paisley, where he took up weaving.

He married Catherine Heywood in 1763, and their son James was born in 1774. James was destined to become a weaver, but after completing an apprenticeship at the age of sixteen, he joined the Ayrshire Fencibles, serving for six years in the south of England. When he was discharged, he walked from London to Paisley, having been given just 2s. 6d. (12 and a half pence) when he left the army.

Back in Paisley, James set up in business as a weaver and in 1802 married Katherine Mitchell, who employed a number of girls tambouring (embroidering) cloth. When ill health forced James to give up weaving, he joined his wife in her trade. He then began manufacturing Canton crepe shawls, which were fashionable at the time. He had bought one for his wife in London and decided to try to make them, as no one

in Scotland did so. The crepe material was made of silk and, as the process required special knowledge and skill, James's first attempts failed. However, when he found that his friend, weaver James Whyte, was also trying to produce the same type of shawl, they went into partnership and mastered the process successfully.

James's entry into manufacturing thread came about through his association with Ross and Duncan, the company that produced the special twisted silk thread required for his shawls. He had become a silent partner in the firm, and as his contract was due to end in 1826, he built his own thread mill in Ferguslie, Paisley, in 1824. He had seen the possibilities for cotton sewing thread and realised that the method of producing it was not much different from that used in producing his shawl yarn.

The message in Coats' advertisement was that the company's thread was reliable and strong. For the sake of the cats in this charming advertisement, let's hope so.

When James retired in 1830, he left the weaving business to his partners and to his son, William. His thread business was taken over by his sons James and Peter, who rented the mill from their father for £500 per annum and formed the partnership of J & P Coats. James and Peter's brother, Thomas, joined the partnership shortly after the firm was set up.

By 1839, the business had prospered and expanded, and as 75 per cent of the thread it produced was exported to the United States, another brother, Andrew, went there to manage sales. Once in the States, he found that Coats' thread was being sold under their American customers' own names instead of the Coats' label. Realising the weaknesses of Coats' selling arrangements, Andrew felt it would be practical to establish the American trade in its own name.

By 1860, Paisley was the most important centre of cotton thread manufacturing in the world, with around a dozen companies involved. Two of these were the largest in the world, J & P Coats and J & J Clark of Seedhill Mills (later Anchor Mills), the leader in the home market, which had begun in 1812.

The agreeable trading situation in the United States ended when the Americans imposed a high import duty on finished thread. They had decided that 'foreigners' should no longer supply them with material for making their garments. To preserve the trade already built up, Coats had no option other than to manufacture in the United States, and in 1870 thread mills at Pawtucket, Rhode Island, were built that grew to be as large as the Ferguslie mills.

With the transfer of the Ferguslie production for the US market to Pawtucket, there was an urgent need for expansion in the British, European and other markets so that the Ferguslie mills' production capacity could be maximised. To this end, Archibald Coats (Peter Coats' son and by the 1870s in charge at Ferguslie under Thomas Coats' general control) managed to increase sales in the home market by concentrating on a few high-quality products such as Coats' standard 200-yard black-and-white six-cord spools for the household trade, together with some other lengths and colours.

These were sold increasingly under the company's 'Chain' trademark. Archibald Coats, however, had little knowledge of foreign markets and relied on the existing system of agencies, which he extended.

Although sales increased greatly, he grew increasingly dissatisfied with the selling system in foreign markets. Consequently, in 1878, he created a new position at Ferguslie – foreign sales manager – to which he appointed Otto Ernst Philippi from the company's Hamburg agency.

The effects of Philippi's appointment were rapid, and he became the focus of dynamic growth in the firm. In 1889, he introduced a joint selling agreement with Coats' main competitor, Clark & Co. This made sense, as competition was fierce, with both companies selling the same articles in the same limited markets worldwide and making narrow profit margins. The agreement, the Sewing Cotton Agency, was formalised a year later as the Central Agency and, as well as

Advertisement of 1952 for Coats Satinised Thread.

Coats and Clark, it included Brook Brothers of Meltham, Yorkshire, a smaller but effective competitor.

Coats became a limited liability company in 1890 with a capital of £5.75 million. While the flotation strengthened the company, competition remained strong worldwide, and in May 1896 Coats and Clark amalgamated, together with Brook Brothers and Chadwick of Eagley Mills, Bolton. The new company took the name of the largest and wealthiest member – J & P Coats – but each arm maintained its own identity. The merger made J & P Coats the largest thread combine in the world.

The period from the amalgamation to the death of chairman Archibald Coats in 1912 was one of stable growth, as world population, real income and demand for clothing and household goods rose, and by 1913 Coats had mills in Russia, Austria, Spain, Belgium, Poland, Hungary, Germany, Italy, Portugal, Switzerland, Brazil, Mexico and Japan. Selling was through the Central Agency Network.

During the First World War, two of the Ferguslie mills produced khaki thread and Egyptian cotton thread for the production of aircraft wings. The Second World War again brought the production of khaki thread, and the company paid an allowance to any of their male workers who joined the armed services. With the men joining up, women took up roles such as drivers and tenters, and some were seconded to other reserve industries. Overtime was prominent, and tea with two buns was supplied during the half-hour tea break.

When life hangs by a thread...
you can depend on Coats

This dramatic example – shows the strength of Coats threads. From this you can realise how they will stand up to all conditions, as well as to the stress and strain of everyday life.
Clothes, carpets, shoes, safety belts, tarpaulins and many other products are all sewn with specially developed Coats threads. Why do manufacturers use Coats threads? Because they're reliable, and because they're backed

by a world famous organisation. Unrivalled as the world's largest thread-makers ... J. & P. Coats have thread depots in 60 countries, factories in 25. With first class materials, intensive research, and the most advanced equipment money can buy ... they leave nothing to chance. That's why Coats threads are always the best!!

○ COATS
the thread makers

156 St. Vincent St., Glasgow C.2.

Advertisement of 1967 for Coats' thread. The theme of this advertisement echoes those of the early days – the reliability and strength of the thread.

The 1960s began with diversification, which, along with trading difficulties in the UK, the emergence of cheap textile products and cheaper labour costs in other countries, contributed to the decline and eventually the demise of thread production in Paisley. In 1961, the merger of Coats with Paton & Baldwin, creating the Coats Paton Group, brought about extensive expansion into the clothing industry with the acquisition of companies such as Jaeger and Pasolds, and producers of children's wear including the Ladybird brand.

Country Casuals, a chain of women's fashion shops, was opened in 1973. With the merger in 1986 of Coats Paton with Vantona Viyella, creating Coats Viyella, products such as carpets and home furnishings (the Dorma brand) were acquired. There were also numerous acquisitions of a non-textile nature. Diversification continued to do the company no favours, and in 1981 the Ferguslie Mill closed along with half of the Anchor Mill, which shut for good in 1993, ending an association with Paisley that had lasted for 181 years.

The twenty-first century started with Coats withdrawing from much of its non-thread making businesses to concentrate of what it always did best, manufacturing and selling thread, a strategy that allows the company to face the future with confidence.

Information and illustrations courtesy of Coats

SCOTCH is the drink

DEWAR'S is the Scotch

No other drink is quite so refreshing as Scotch Whisky. You can drink it short or long, as the mood takes you, but whether served neat or with a cold draught of iced water, or with soda, Scotch is the friendliest drink of all. Have a Dewar's "White Label", a very fine Scotch indeed, when next you have a thirst.

DEWAR'S "White Label" SCOTCH WHISKY
–it never varies

SCOTLAND'S PRIDE—
THE WORLD'S CHOICE

After the difficult trading climate of the Second World War the business had a resurgence in the 1950s. Their marketing during this period, much of it aimed at the export market, was quintessentially Scottish depicting a proud marching soldier in full regalia.

26

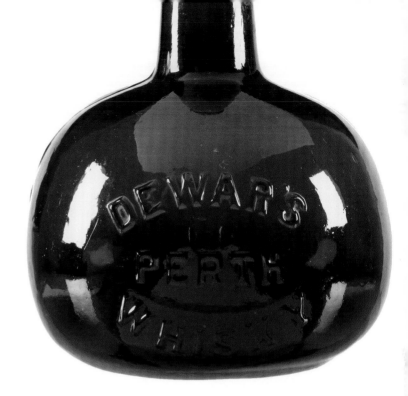

Glass bottle that John Dewar used for his blends instead of kegs or stone jars as was the custom.

John Dewar & Sons

John Dewar & Sons produce the biggest selling Scotch whisky in the US, and its Dewar's 12 is the fastest growing deluxe whisky in the world.

Dewar's origins go back to John Dewar, born in 1805 in the small village of Dull, near Aberfeldy.

After leaving school he was apprenticed to a joiner, after which he joined his relative Alex MacDonald's wine and spirits business in Perth as a cellarman. In 1846, he decided to start his own business, and in a little shop at 111 High Street, Perth, he set up as a wine and spirit merchant. The business flourished, and he began blending his own whisky from several different producers to give it a mellower flavour.

In 1871, one of Dewar's ten children, John Alexander, joined the business, and in 1879, at the age of 23, he became a partner. A year later John Dewar senior died and John junior, a skilled whisky blender as well as a talented businessman, took over the firm. Round about 1884, John's brother, 20-year-old Tommy, joined the

firm, having been trained in Leith and Glasgow with Robertson & Baxter, the well-known firm of wine and spirit merchants. When Tommy became a partner a few years later, he persuaded his brother to go for the English market. Having a knack for marketing, Tommy set off for London in 1885 with introductions to only two men, one of whom he discovered was dead and the other bankrupt. Despite this setback, through hard work and determination, Tommy managed to create a demand for Dewar's whisky.

In 1890, Tommy secured an exclusive contract to supply Scotch whisky to top catering firm Spiers and Pond, whose customers included railway buffets, hotels and music venues. It was said that Tommy was probably more responsible than anyone else for the success of Scotch whisky in London.

Dewar's business flourished, and in order to ensure supplies of whisky, the firm leased the Tullymet distillery in Ballinluig, south-east of Pitlochry, from the Duke of Atholl. It also purchased a bonded warehouse at Speygate in Perth, and in 1898 Dewar's built a new distillery at Aberfeldy. In 1899, what was to become Dewar's most popular blend, White Label, was introduced.

In 1915, John Dewar & Sons merged with the large whisky blending firm of James Buchanan to form a holding company, Scotch Whisky Brands Ltd, that in 1919 was renamed Buchanan-Dewar. In 1923, to ensure supplies of whisky for blending, the company bought distilleries at Ord, Parkmore, Pulteney and Aultmore.

In 1925, along with John Walker & Sons Ltd, Buchanan-Dewar merged with the Distillers Company Ltd (DCL), created in 1877 by a merger of six distillers. John and Tommy Dewar joined the board of DCL.

In 1900 the Dewar brothers had been elected to Parliament, Tommy representing the Conservatives and John the Liberals. Tommy received a knighthood in 1901 and John a baronetcy in 1907. In 1917 John had become Baron Forteviot of Dupplin, the first of the 'Whisky Barons'. In 1919 Tommy became Baron Dewar of Homestall.

John Dewar died in November 1929 and Tommy in April 1930, and their work was carried on by Peter Dewar, not a relative, who was chairman of the company from 1930 to 1946. It was he who saw it through the difficult days of the Second World War.

By 1980, Dewar's White Label had become the top-selling whisky in the United States. In 1986, Guinness acquired the Distillers Company and John Dewar & Sons in a hostile takeover. In 1998 Bacardi bought Dewar's, amalgamating it with its other whisky brand, William Lawson's.

In 2000, Dewar's introduced its premium product, Dewar's 12-Year-Old Scotch whisky blend, now the fastest growing deluxe whisky in the world. It also opened Dewar's World of Whisky, a £2 million visitor's centre, at the Aberfeldy distillery.

More than a century and a half after its founder began blending whisky in Perth, Dewar continues to produce fine distilled beverages, and Dewar's expanded portfolio includes Dewar's 18-Year-Old, Dewar's Signature, and Aberfeldy 12-Year-Old and 21-Year-Old single malt whiskies.

Information and illustrations courtesy Dewar & Sons

Advertisement c.1930s entitled 'The Spirit of Give and Take'. The illustration was the work of Geoffrey Squire, who painted many of Dewar's advertisements at the time.

This 1950s' advertisement highlights the origins of Drambuie by portraying a member of the MacKinnon clan blending rare herbs according to the secret recipe in the Isle of Skye during the eighteenth century.

Mist-shrouded isles, heather-covered hills, a handsome prince, loyal followers, mystery, murder and intrigue! A synopsis for a film script or a novel? No, it's that of a true story – the incredible ancestry of Drambuie, the only British liqueur to be exported to every major world market.

Drambuie, a combination of whiskies blended with herbal essence and heather honey, owes its origins to Prince Charles Edward Stuart and Captain John MacKinnon, a native of the Isle of Skye, and a fervent supporter of the Jacobite cause.

With the defeat at Culloden in 1746, the Prince's aspirations of gaining a crown vanished. His small army of poorly-equipped Highlanders stood no chance against the Duke of Cumberland's forces.

After the battle, no mercy was shown to the Jacobites, and the Duke more than earned his title of 'Butcher Cumberland'.

Although Charles had a price on his head of £30,000, no one betrayed him, and for five months a

IT TRAVELS WELL

THE DRAMBUIE LIQUEUR COMPANY LTD, EDINBURGH, SCOTLAND.

One of the luxurious art-deco-style Drambuie advertisements devised to convey how far afield the product travelled by showing a sophisticated couple on what looks like the Orient Express enjoying a Drambuie.

small band of friends sheltered him until he was smuggled aboard a ship for France, never to return to Scotland. John MacKinnon was one of those who never left the Prince's side, and as a reward for his loyalty, the Prince gave him the secret recipe for his personal liqueur – all he had of value. It is not known from where the recipe came. It is known, however, that when he was on the run in Scotland, the Prince had a little bottle in his pouch out of which he used to take drops every morning and throughout the day, saying that if anything should ail him he hoped he should cure himself, for he was something of a doctor. It was common in Europe for people to drink elixirs for ailments – usually a strong spirit to which special mixtures of spices and herbs were added to the specific direction of an individual. Despite no clear evidence as to the origins of the liqueur recipe given to MacKinnon by the Prince, it is feasible it was that of his personal elixir.

Although the exact ingredients and quantities that make the Drambuie liqueur of today are a well-guarded secret, there is an idea of what went into its forerunner, as fragments of ancient recipes exist.

The MacKinnons' liqueur remained for personal use until 1871 when John Ross, who owned the inn at Broadford, Skye, persuaded one of the MacKinnons to let him try making it and selling it in the inn. The result was much appreciated by the regulars, two of whom were said to declare it to be *an dram buidheach* – 'the drink that satisfies'.

Although in 1893 John Ross's son James registered the trademark 'Drambuie', (derived from *an dram buidheach*), there was no commercialisation of the liqueur until 1909. Malcolm MacKinnon, who had left Skye in 1900 to work for the Edinburgh wholesale wine and spirit merchant W. MacBeth and Son, met Eleanor, James Ross's widow, who had moved to Edinburgh after her husband's death. Eleanor had kept the recipe given to her husband by the MacKinnons, and Malcolm thought that the old liqueur might be ideal to revitalise the MacBeth business of which he had become a partner. He therefore reached an agreement with Mrs Ross to manufacture and sell Drambuie, and to have the trademark assigned to MacBeth.

Malcolm was taking a gamble by introducing a new whisky drink when he did. Whisky sales had collapsed when, in his 1909 'People's Budget', Chancellor Lloyd George, a confirmed teetotaller, increased whisky excise duty by a third and taxed distilleries direct for the amount of whisky they produced. So draconian were the increases, that one of MacBeth's competitors declared that he might as well close his doors.

While in Drambuie's first year only 12 cases were sold, demand grew, and from Malcolm's initial production of 12 bottles a fortnight, the company progressed to exporting cases to military regiments and expatriate Scots the world over. This was achieved by heavily investing in advertising, which Malcolm had realised was necessary to market a new product. He cleverly focused on the age and the romantic story of the liqueur, which he thought would make it distinguished and memorable.

Advertisements in trade papers and respected publications such as the *Tatler*, *The Times*, *Punch*, the *Sketch* and the *Bystander* had images of Bonnie Prince Charlie and Highland scenery accompanied by wording emphasising how Drambuie had been known in the

Highlands since 1745 and was only now being offered to a wider public. It was described as 'The Isle of Skye Liqueur'. Malcolm also devised a unique squat bottle intended to make Drambuie stand out among a shelf full of traditional whiskies.

Drambuie was the first liqueur to be accepted in the cellars of the Houses of Parliament, as well as into those of the royal household at Buckingham Palace. By the end of the First World War, every British officers' mess and naval wardroom had its stock of Drambuie, and in the United States sales soared when the era of Prohibition ended.

In 1937, the Drambuie Liqueur Company Limited took over the old-established whisky blender Innes and Grieve, whose premises were at 12 York Place, Edinburgh. Drambuie's production was moved into these premises, but that was all that changed. The quality of the product remained true to the original recipe, which is kept in a safe deposit box in an Edinburgh bank. The recipe for the essence is still a closely guarded secret, and even today a female member of the Mackinnon family blends the ingredients in a private laboratory.

When ready, the essence is transferred into custom-built containers that are double padlocked. Only one employee is entrusted with a key, and that person is responsible for the blending of the essence with the whisky base.

Drambuie again had a monopoly in the liqueur market in Britain during the Second World War, as continental brands were unavailable, as they had been in the previous war. Supplies were available in pubs and hotels as well as in regimental messes, and as the Allied forces gathered in the south of England in 1944, there were sufficient reserves for the troops. By this time, Malcolm MacKinnon was seriously ill, and in May 1945, at the age of sixty-two, he died.

After the war there was an increased worldwide demand for Drambuie, and in 1959 a new production facility was opened at Easter Road, Edinburgh, and although the plant was technologically advanced, the herbs and spices were still collected and mixed by one person, Gina MacKinnon, Malcolm's widow and the chairman of the company.

Growth continued, and in 1969 work began on another new plant at Kirkliston, eight miles west of Edinburgh. While it was the most advanced and sophisticated liqueur-processing plant in the world, the production process was a careful balance between technology and traditional values, including the time-honoured practice of rinsing out bottles with a jet of pure whisky before use.

The brilliant Nectar advertisement showing a hummingbird hovering to capture the elusive drop of Drambuie.

Nectar

By the 1970s, however, the whisky industry was in turmoil, with even a successful brand like Drambuie fighting to maintain sales. As Malcolm MacKinnon had done years before, heavily investing in marketing and promotion was the solution, and advertisements geared to an international customer base, such as the luxurious Art-Deco-style series with the slogan 'It Travels Well', appeared in magazines and Sunday newspaper supplements. These successful advertisements, along with the brilliant 'Nectar' one, showing a hummingbird hovering to capture the elusive drop of Drambuie, gave the liqueur a sophisticated rather than a homespun image.

A 2002 advertisement for Drambuie on ice.

There are after dinner drinks

And there's Drambuie.

DRAMBUIE ON ICE.

Television advertising did not begin until 1990, when a humorous approach was adopted. In the first advertisement, the clumsy butler who drops the Drambuie sets in motion an intercontinental journey for a replacement, which he promptly drops again to the exasperation of actor Robert Hardy.

Drambuie breaks all language barriers and is the quintessential Scottish liqueur, epitomising quality, refinement and taste. It mixes well, making it the perfect partner in classic and contemporary cocktails, like the 'Rusty Nail' – a combination of quality Scotch and Drambuie. Its sophisticated strength and subtlety is superb over cubed or crushed ice, a combination promoted in a sequel to the hapless butler television advertisement, this time featuring actor Robert Powell at his Venetian dinner party requesting ice from the Alps to add to the Drambuie.

Most of the Drambuie Liqueur Company's sales are now to the export market. The product is truly international and can be found in over 200 countries, in duty-free outlets, planes, boats and trains. If you travel abroad, therefore, you can enjoy Drambuie before departure, in transit and at your journey's end.

As by the twenty-first century the Kirkliston plant was in need of updating, Drambuie formed a supply chain partnership with Glenmorangie, a distiller of premium malt whiskies. A new company, Glenaird Ltd, was formed to handle Glenmorangie's and Drambuie's supply chains, and in the summer of 2001 Drambuie's bottling operations were transferred to Glenmorangie's plant at Broxburn. Throughout the process, both companies emphasised that they intend to retain their independence.

In 2014 Drambuie was sold to William Grant & Sons, the maker of Glenfiddich whisky, who will carry on the extraordinary Drambuie story and keep alive the Gaelic motto that appeared on every bottle of Drambuie, which says: *Cuimhnich An Tabhartas Prionsa* – 'Remember the Gift of the Prince'.

Information and illustrations courtesy of Drambuie

09

'On the floor of this drawing-room is Nairn Super Parquet Inlaid Linoleum. It is not only artistic, hardwearing and resilient, but, when polished, makes an admirable dancing floor.'

The name of Kirkcaldy has become synonymous with the production of linoleum, and at the forefront of the industry that brought prosperity to the Lang Toun is the floor-covering giant Forbo-Nairn Limited, or Nairn's as it has been to Kirkcaldy folk since 1847, when Michael Nairn started building the 'Scottish Floor Cloth Manufactory'.

In 1828, at the age of twenty-eight, Michael Nairn, from a long-established Fife family, started up a canvas-weaving business in Coal Wynd, Kirkcaldy. His wares were mainly used for sailcloth and as well as selling them in Britain, he exported to the corners of the world. Bleached canvas went to India, Canada, America, Jamaica, Australia, Mauritius and even Greenland. Also to America went oilcloth – canvas that has been waterproofed.

Times were changing, however, and, with the arrival of steam power, so was the shipping industry. The days of sail were numbered, and sales to floorcloth manufacturers gradually played a larger role in Michael Nairn's operations until, by 1844, he was supplying

Hand-printing loft for floorcloth. This illustration gives an indication of what a hand-printing department was like in the nineteenth century. The boys shown were known as 'tear boys'. This name, variously spelt, was taken from the old word 'teer', which meant to spread, to plaster, to daub. This exactly described the work of the boys, who spread paint over a large pad composed of three-ply plaiding covered by a piece of canvas. (Michael Nairn had been supplying these pads to English floorcloth factories for years.) The name 'tear boy' was not confined to floorcloth making. It was current in other industries where a similar block-printing process was used.

canvas to two dozen floorcloth firms, two-thirds of the total number in existence. The canvas was used as backing for the floorcloth.

Although developed in the seventeenth century, floorcloth was made mainly in London, with no factories outside England. Michael Nairn decided to change that. After visiting one of his customers, John Hare of Bristol, he returned to Kirkcaldy in a thoughtful mood. As he was already equipped to make floorcloth canvas, why should he not produce floorcloth? As the manufacturing process took as long as ten months from start to finish, however, it would be a tremendous gamble as he would have to start from scratch by building a factory, buying materials, paying workers and keeping everything going with no money coming in for two years.

When Michael began to look for partners among his friends so that he could set up his floorcloth factory, they all thought he was mad and declined to be involved.

Nevertheless, in 1847, he started work on a new factory on a site at the top of a cliff at Pathhead near Ravenscraig Castle. Little did his friends know, however, that a completely new manufacturing era had arrived. Even Michael, ambitious though he was, could hardly have had an inkling that he was laying the foundations of a business that would reach out across the world and would still be thriving in the twenty-first century.

In 1849, the first floorcloth was ready for sale. Making it was an involved process. Two men wove a canvas web 150 yards long by eight yards wide in a fortnight. The web was then cut into 25-yard lengths that were nailed taut on to vertical frames to stretch before sizing and painting. There was no question of buying in paint – the workers made their own. Combinations of ochres and leads were ground to a powder and mixed with linseed oil and various other ingredients, and then ground again between a pair of millstones. Several coats of the thick paint were daubed on to the canvas with brushes and spread with trowels into a thin film. Once each coat of paint was dry, it was rubbed smooth with pumice stone. The processes took months to complete as the only way of drying the paint was by ventilation through the factory's huge 41-foot-high windows. The first floor was 47 feet high, so 90-foot lengths of linoleum could be suspended in giant U shapes to dry. Then came the printing. Designs in 18-inch square blocks were printed repeatedly, with additional colours or elaborate patterns being overprinted with different blocks.

For some time, floorcloth had been criticised for being too cold underfoot, and in 1863, Yorkshireman Frederick Walton registered a patent for linoleum, a warmer and more resilient alternative.

Although linoleum was initially made in one-yard widths, making it in many respects inferior to the much wider floorcloth, Michael Barker Nairn, Michael Nairn's son, believed it had a future. He bided his time until Walton's patent ran out, and in 1877, having constructed a purpose-built factory, started producing linoleum.

At first the linoleum was made in two-yard widths and had to be hand-printed, then in 1881 Nairn, now run by Michael Barker Nairn, was the first to produce it in four-yard widths. The printed designs were still a drawback, but in 1895 a major development came with the introduction of inlaid designs, which meant the pattern went right through the linoleum.

Although in the 1950s Nairn successfully introduced Lino Tiles, by the following decade linoleum was out of favour. PVC and vinyl floor coverings had come on to the market, as had cheap tufted carpets manufactured by companies such as Cyril Lord, whose adverts told everyone that 'this was the luxury you could afford'. Everyone wanted wall-to-wall carpeting, and Britain became the most carpeted country in the world per capita.

Sales of printed vinyl kept Nairn going, but it was an invention by American subsidiary Congoleum-Nairn – Cushionflor – a cushioned vinyl, which, when launched in 1967, proved to be the company's salvation, as by 1972 it was Britain's most popular resilient floor-covering.

Cushionflor did not mean the end for linoleum – Nairn continued to manufacture it despite annual sales having fallen from 21 million square metres in 1965 to just 1.78 million by 1981. Help, however, was around the corner in the form of Swiss based Forbo SA, which had faith in linoleum and produced it in Holland. Forbo wanted a base in the UK, and when Unilever, which owned Nairn, decided to sell up in 1985, Forbo-Nairn was born, giving Kirkcaldy's linoleum industry a new lease of life. Because linoleum is a generic term, not a brand name, Forbo-Nairn's product is known as Marmoleum.

Environmentally friendly Marmoleum is the latest in designer flooring. Using aquajet cutters, floor design is limited only by the customer's imagination. Any image can be created, like Sonic the Hedgehog for Sega World in London. Other commercial customers go for more discreet company logos. Children's hospitals have teddies and cartoons, and Forbo-Nairn's own offices are an eye-catching advertisement for the company.

With two such quality products as Cushionflor and Marmoleum, Forbo-Nairn, the oldest manufacturer of resilient floor-coverings in the world, should go from strength to strength. Michael Nairn's gamble certainly paid off.

Information and illustrations courtesy of Forbo-Nairn Archive

This image of 1968 is the front page of the first Cushionflor brochure.

Glenfiddich stills, which have not changed in shape or size from the originals. Even the original dents incurred on the journey from Cardhu to Glenfiddich were carefully replicated in case the spirit would be affected.

10

Glenfiddich®

The story of Glenfiddich, the world's best-selling malt whisky and the world's first single malt whisky, is fascinating.

The distillery, which has been continuously owned and managed by the Grant family for five generations, began with William Grant, born in 1839, the son of a Dufftown tailor who had served with Wellington in the Penninsular Wars.

The young William Grant was first a cattle-herder, then an apprentice cobbler and finally a clerk at the local lime works, before joining the nearby Mortlach distillery in 1866 as book-keeper and later manager. During his twenty years at Mortlach, William learned all he could about distilling as he had decided that his future lay in establishing his own distillery. To this end, the family saved every penny it could – William from his £200 a year salary, his wife from frugal housekeeping, his children from university prizes and, in

the case of his eldest son, John, from his teacher's salary. William had nine children – two daughters and seven sons – all of whom were allowed to study, unusual for the times. Among the family were a teacher, a lawyer and two doctors.

After years of saving, William had a lucky break in 1886. When the Cardhu Distillery at Knockando decided to install a new plant, he acquired the old plant for the bargain price of £119 19s. 0d (approximately £45,000 in today's money). William then chose a site close to Dufftown in the field of Glenfiddich for his distillery. Water was to be drawn from the Robbie Dhu Springs in the Conval Hills, a secret location that legend says was shown to William by a priest.

Working seven days a week, with just the help of a mason, a carpenter and the advice of an architect, William and his family built their distillery for little more than £700. Named 'Glenfiddich', the first whisky ran from its stills on Christmas Day 1887. As well as helping to finance the distillery, William's children helped run it, even his three youngest sons who were still at school preparing for entrance to Aberdeen University.

The bulk of Glenfiddich's whisky was sold for blending. It was also sold as being suitable for medicinal purposes, the justification being, according to the company, that every stage of it was supervised by a qualified doctor – William's fourth son, Alex, who was the head stillman. His younger brother George was maltman, and Charles was the brewer.

A big breakthrough came when Smith's Glenlivet Distillery caught fire and Glenfiddich was able to step in and meet an order that Glenlivet could not fulfil. After that the company prospered, and by 1892 it was building a second distillery at nearby Balvenie.

When William Grant sent both his son Charles and son-in-law Charles Gordon to Glasgow to establish a base from which to wholesale and export the William Grant blended whisky brand, it took Charles Gordon 181 calls to make his first sale. Later he travelled to the Far East, Australia and New Zealand while John Grant travelled to Canada and the United States. Their efforts were rewarded, as by the beginning of the First World War William Grant was selling its blends

Advertisement from The Glenfiddich Guide to the Seven Deadly Sins series – 4 'Lust'.

worldwide through sixty agencies in thirty countries.

Despite going blind, William Grant carried on the business he and his family had worked so hard to build up, and he was eighty-three when he died in 1923.

Most Glenfiddich whisky was sold for blending, that is until 1963 when a courageous decision was made to market Glenfiddich as a single malt whisky. It was a gamble, as single malt whisky had never been generally promoted as it was considered too strong in flavour and body. Glenfiddich, however, was a delicately flavoured light-bodied whisky so it was a success, and by 1974 almost 120,000 cases were being exported. Glenfiddich created the malt whisky market.

Unlike any other producer, all the water used at Glenfiddich is from a single source – the Robbie Dhu Springs – hence the marketing slogan 'a single source of inspiration'. William Grant would find little changed at Glenfiddich since his time. The same raw materials are still used in the making of the whisky because to alter a single detail might affect the taste and quality of Glenfiddich, something the company is not prepared to risk.

Since 1886, the single-minded dedication of William Grant & Sons Ltd has resulted in it producing the finest single malt Scotch whisky in the world. 'Made without Compromise' appears on the label of Special Reserve, the world's best-selling single malt whisky. These words sum up the philosophy of the company.

Information and illustrations courtesy of William Grant & Sons

11

In the UK, the bottled water market is worth £2.4 billion, with 3.3 billion litres consumed in 2018.

More than half of the adult population drinks bottled water, a very different story from when mineral waters were considered medicines, which they were until 1833, when they were exempted from levies and could be drunk for refreshment as well as for medicinal purposes.

Formed in 1979, Highland Spring is the leading UK-produced brand of bottled water and the number one spring water. Its home is the village of Blackford in Perthshire, which has been renowned for its water for centuries. King James IV stopped there in 1488 and paid the, then, vast sum of 12 shillings (60p) for ale made from local water.

Highland Spring's water, which is low in minerals, salts and nitrates, comes from a natural underground source under the Ochil Hills, where no farming, agricultural spraying, building or habitation are permitted within the 2000-acre catchment area. The land has been kept free from pesticides and pollution for over twenty years.

The weather on the Ochil Hills is harsh. Even on a mild autumn day, the temperature at the top of the Hills can drop to minus zero, and when it rains, it rains sideways.

Although every drop helps to replenish the reservoirs deep underground, there is no problem with supply, as Highland Spring only uses a fraction of the water in the hillside. The water, regarded by experts to be among the finest mineral waters in the world, takes about fifteen years to filter through the basalt and sandstone strata to boreholes lined with stainless steel, which allow the water to be gently pumped to the surface and then down to the bottling plant. Mineral water must be bottled at source, and at Highland Spring it is bottled within hours of leaving the

The Ochil Hills in summer.

ground. It is untouched by human hand and is delivered to consumers exactly as nature intended, with nothing added or taken away (apart from the addition of CO2 for its sparkling range).

Research shows that British consumers view Scotland as having the purest water in the UK, and Highland Spring's stylised tartan packaging highlights the product's Scottish provenance.

In April 2001, Highland Spring acquired its Blackford neighbour, Gleneagles Spring Water Company, an upmarket brand of natural mineral water with an award-winning stylish glass bottle. The water is bottled at source from the Gleneagles valley in the Ochil Hills. Popular in exclusive hotels and restaurants, at home and abroad, it is the only natural mineral water brand stocked by the Scotch Whisky Heritage Centre. The company also owns Watermedia, the UK market leader in the niche private sector label.

Despite a growth in the popularity of bottled water amongst youngsters, carbonated drinks remain their most popular choice, and in 2007 the company launched the first sparkling kids' water, Highland Spring for Kids, now the leading brand of children's bottled water.

Still water accounts for around 76 per cent of bottled water sales, and Highland Spring out-performed the bottled water market in 2017. It consolidated its number two position by extending its lead over the third largest brand, Volvic, while edging closer to Evian. In the sparkling market, Highland Spring is the market leader, and it sells five times more than its nearest competitor, Perrier.

Highland Spring is a major supporter of UK sport and a long-term sponsor of many national and international events, such as the Johnnie Walker Golf Championship and the Paralympic World Cup. It was the exclusive beverage sponsor of Andy Murray, Britain's number one tennis player, who displayed the brand logo on his shirt sleeve and drank Highland Spring as part of his dietary regime before he retired from the sport in 2019. It is also the official bottled water supplier to the World Snooker Association and sponsor of Team Highland Spring, which consists of 14 snooker players, including Stephen Hendry, Ronnie O'Sullivan and Ken Doherty. The Highland Spring logo and tartan appears on the players' waistcoats.

As people are becoming more aware of the health benefits of drinking water, such as lubricating joints,

Colourful advertisement from 2005 showing a bottle of Highland Spring water depicted as a stylised thistle.

regulating blood pressure and boosting skin health, the sharp rise in global demand for bottled water looks set to continue.

To facilitate increased demand, Highland Spring was reclassified as a 'spring water' in 2007 to enable it to manage its water resources more efficiently, and to give access to at least another 100 million litres of water a year, without putting stress on the catchment area or local environment.

Information and illustrations courtesy of Highland Spring

DID YOU KNOW?

In 1985, Highland Spring was recognised as a 'natural mineral water' under EU legislation.

It was in 1993 that Highland Spring really took off, when British Airways picked it as their chosen water.

Highland Spring became the first British beverage producer to be recognised for its environmental efforts, achieving EMAS accreditation in 2001.

By 2004, Highland Spring had become the No. 1 sparkling water brand in the UK.

In 2013, The Sunday Times Rich List named Mahdi al-Tajir, owner of Highland Spring, Scotland's richest man.

Early Iron Brew label featuring Highland athlete Adam Brown.

12

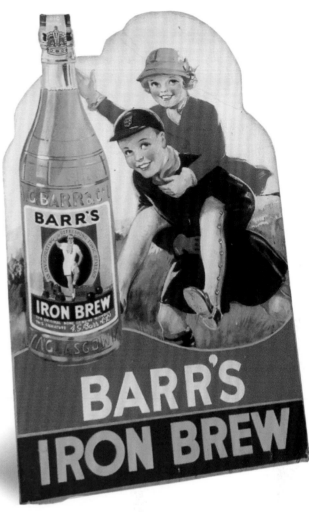

Irn-Bru is the leading brand of soft drink manufacturer A. G. Barr plc.

Known as 'Scotland's other national drink' and a favourite hangover cure for Glaswegians, the recipe is a secret known to only two board members and is kept in a bank vault for safety. What makes the recipe unique is that, while other carbonated fruit drinks typically have at most two or three flavouring ingredients, Irn-Bru has thirty-two, which is why it has proved impossible to copy.

The Barr story began in 1875 when Robert Barr added a soft drinks business to the cork-cutting operations established by his father in Falkirk in 1830. In 1887, Robert's son, also named Robert, started his own soft drinks business in Great Eastern Road, Glasgow, later renamed Gallowgate. Five years after getting his business up and running, however, Robert

moved to Ireland, leaving his brother Andrew as sole proprietor, at which time the company became A. G. Barr & Co.

In 1901, Robert Barr, Falkirk, and A. G. Barr & Co., Glasgow, jointly launched Iron Brew, just one of many such named products – a refreshing mixed-flavour drink for which all the manufacturers had their own recipes. When Iron Brew was introduced, A. G. Barr employed around 200 people in Glasgow and 150 horses were required to cope with deliveries. As it is today, advertising was important, and Andrew Barr gave his lorries eye-catching white and gold livery carrying the company name in large clear letters.

At the start of the Second World War Iron Brew remained on sale, but in 1942, because of a shortage

A late 1930s' example of point-of-sale material used for 'Iron Brew'.

of raw materials like sugar and paper, the government restricted the industry to a number of manufacturers. Each one authorised to continue was given a number. Barr's was 'No. 6'. However, the companies were allowed to manufacture only standard drinks, and as Iron Brew was not recognised as one of these, production of that flavour ceased. The company advertised the loss of Iron Brew during the war as 'One of the hardships of the war effort'!

1930s' Iron Brew poster featuring 'Ba-Bru'.

When, after the war, it was proposed to introduce new food-labelling regulations that stipulated that brand names should be literally true, there was concern that the name Iron Brew would no longer be permitted. Just as Ginger Ale was not ale and American Cream Soda was neither made in America nor contained cream, Iron Brew was not brewed, although it did contain 0.125 mg of iron per fluid ounce. Chairman Robert Barr's brilliant idea to get round this legislation was to use a phonetic version of the generic name, and in 1946 'Irn-Bru' was registered as the trade name for the company's No. 1 brand.

The Barr story is not one of spectacular growth but of steady expansion, careful acquisition and persistent specialisation. In 1954, the company set out to 'conquer' England by acquiring John Hollows, a small company based in Bradford, and an advertising campaign to introduce Irn-Bru to the north of England was launched. In 1959, one single-family business was finally created when A. G. Barr & Co. took over the original Robert Barr business in Falkirk.

Barr's products were sold in Edinburgh for the first time in only 1963. When Robert Barr had set up his soft drinks business in Falkirk in 1875, Mr Dunbar of the Dunbar soft drinks company in Edinburgh helped him to do so, leading to a gentleman's agreement that neither company would sell their products in each other's territory. This agreement, which lasted for over eighty-five years, ended only when Dunbar bought a soft drinks business in Kirkcaldy where Barr was already established.

In 1965, A. G. Barr & Co. Ltd was floated on the Stock Exchange, with 500,000 ordinary shares being offered for sale at 9s. 3d (approximately £11.00 in today's money). Applications for over two million shares were received. After the flotation, the company expanded its business south with the acquisition of

MADE IN SCOTLAND FROM GIRDERS.

An advertisement from the mid-1970s featuring 'Popeye' consuming a can of Irn-Bru to give him strength instead of his customary spinach.

An amusing, but suggestive, poster from 2001.

"THERE'S NOTHING BETTER THAN IRN-BRU WHEN YOU'VE JUST BEEN LAID."

WWW.IRN-BRU.CO.UK

soft drink companies in Sunderland and Atherton, near Manchester. Special Irn-Bru labels were produced for the English market.

Barr's breakthrough nationally came in 1972 when it acquired Tizer Ltd, the proprietors of the famous household brand 'Tizer the Appetizer'. Expansion continued in the 1980s with the purchase of Globe Soft Drinks of Edinburgh and Mandora St. Clements with factories in Mansfield and Evesham.

Innovative, witty and vigorous advertising has always played a large part in Irn-Bru's success, and while early advertising focused on associating sporting and athletic prowess with the company's products, the 1930s saw the introduction of the company's well-loved campaign that introduced generations of Scots to Barr's Iron Brew. It was the 'Adventures of Ba-Bru and Sandy', two boys, one a turbaned Indian, one a tam-o-shantered, kilted Scot, forever on the hunt for Barr's Iron Brew. ('Ba-Bru' was inspired by the character Sabu in Rudyard Kipling's book *Sabu the Elephant Boy*.)

The well-loved Ba-Bru and Sandy gave way to a more sophisticated style of advertising in the mid-1970s – the highly successful poster and TV campaign that coined the famous catchphrases 'Your other national drink' and 'Made in Scotland from girders'.

Boys with ginger hair were used while the metal girders symbolised the iron. Characters symbolising strength, such as 'Popeye', were also used. Although these campaigns ended in the 1990s, people still remember the famous phrases. Barr's sugar tankers, painted to look like giant Irn-Bru cans, bore the slogan 'Don't drink more than eighty gallons a day or you'll rust.'

Irn-Bru is as Scottish as tartan and shortbread, and is among the most popular Scottish products craved by ex-pats the world over. It was 100 years old in 2001 and is the No. 1 grocery brand in Scotland. From being just one of hundreds of soft drinks businesses in Scotland in 1875, A. G. Barr is the UK's No. 1 independent soft drinks business with 980 employees working from 11 sites.

Information and illustrations courtesy of A. G. Barr p.l.c.

JOHNNIE WALKER

BORN 1820

STILL GOING STRONG

In 1908 Tom Browne, a famous commercial artist of the day, was commissioned to draw a cheery Regency figure to represent the company's founder. What became know as the Striding Man figure advert along with the slogan 'Johnnie Walker born 1820' were registered in 1910. It was to become one of the most endurtng advertisement campaigns ever devised.

<u>13</u>

In 1820 John Walker, son of an Ayrshire farmer, opened a small grocery, wine and spirit shop in Kilmarnock. He became a blending pioneer and was soon selling his own stocks of whisky all over the surrounding area.

From the beginning, John's blend had a high reputation that spread throughout Scotland, and eventually into England. His son, Alexander, joined him in 1856 and moved the company in the direction of wholesale rather than retail trade. John Walker died in 1857.

While the blend 'Johnnie Walker's Old Highland Whisky' was begun in the 1850s, the label was not copyrighted until 1867. Old Highland, which became known as 'Walker's Kilmarnock Whisky', was a long way in character and taste from modern Scotch, but it was in its day a most successful product – extremely rich and peaty with a very strong taste. The secret blend recipe still exists.

Ambitious Alexander reached overseas markets by entrusting his whisky to the captains of ships sailing out of Glasgow who sold it on commission at the best price they could get. He also took advantage of Kilmarnock's reputation as a carpet and textile centre to introduce the visiting English buyers to the delights of his whisky. Having done that, he made sure they could get their supplies at home by opening a London office in 1880.

When Alexander Walker died in 1889, Johnnie Walker & Sons Limited was one of the most important whisky firms in the world. After Alexander's death, his three sons, George, John and Alexander, took over. In 1890, when John Walker sailed for Australia where he opened the company's first overseas subsidiary, local man James Stevenson joined the firm and went on to play an outstanding part in its growth and expansion.

1905 sales card for John Walker & Sons Old Highland Whiskies.

As demand for whisky was soaring worldwide, to increase production and to maintain the quality of its product, the firm needed its own distillery. In 1893, therefore, it acquired the once illegal distillery of Cardhu in Speyside, so highly rated by the Walker brothers' father that he used its malt whisky as the base around which he developed his Old Highland blend. At the same time, a new director was acquired, John Cumming, son of Elizabeth Cumming who sold Cardhu to the Walkers. The purchase guaranteed the firm the supply of the finest Highland whiskies that it needed for its blends, a fact it emphasised: 'The purchase of the distillery will give us a thorough command of our manufacture from the very start and give us absolute certainty about the quality of the principal components of our blend.'

In the early 1900s, the firm decided to replace its two principal blends, Johnnie Walker Very Special Old Highland Whisky and Johnnie Walker Extra Special Old Highland Whisky, with new ones that would build on the traditional taste and quality, but have fresh dimensions of complexity and subtlety. To this end, Alexander Walker, who was a master blender, and two blending experts, set to work and produced the famous Johnnie Walker Red Label and Johnnie Walker Black Label whiskies. It is interesting to note that Johnnie Walker whiskies taste exactly the same today as they did when created. Buy a bottle of Red Label or Black Label and you will experience the flavour that so excited Alexander Walker and his co-blenders when it was first sampled. Why change a winning formula?

In the case of Red Label, all the ingredient whiskies were older than the three years that was legally necessary for a whisky to be described as Scotch. With Black Label, Alexander turned to older stocks of whisky that had been matured for more than twelve years. Even today, only the master blender and one or two of his colleagues have access to the original recipes, all of which remain closely guarded secrets. The name 'Walker's Kilmarnock Whisky' was dropped and replaced by the brand name 'Johnnie Walker'. New distinctive red and black labels set at a slant across a square bottle were adopted, as was the 'Striding Man' figure trademark and the slogan 'Johnnie Walker born 1820 – still going strong'.

Registered in 1910, the Striding Man figure and slogan had come about

Time Marches On. An advertisement from 1948 in which Johnnie Walker says he was proud to have seen the paddle-boat become the 'Queen' – the liner Queen Elizabeth.

TIME MARCHES ON!

It makes me proud to think I've seen
The paddle-boat become the "Queen."
Like Clyde-built ships, I've grown in fame
The skill behind me's still the same.

JOHNNIE WALKER
SCOTCH WHISKY
Born 1820 –
still going
strong

in 1908 when it was decided to incorporate a portrait of the firm's founder into an advertising scheme. Tom Browne, a celebrated commercial artist, was commissioned to draw a cheerful Regency figure, complete with top hat, eyeglass and cane, striding out purposefully. Alongside the finished sketch, director James Stevenson scribbled the famous slogan 'Johnnie Walker born 1820 – still going strong'. It was one of the most successful advertising promotions devised and made the name 'Johnnie Walker' universally known. The original sketch was miraculously rescued from Walker's premises, which were bombed during the Second World War, and remains a prized possession of the company.

By 1920, Johnnie Walker was one of the three top whisky companies in the world, the others being Dewar and Buchanan. (Walker's went public in 1923 and in 1925 Walker, Dewar and Buchanan became part of the Distillers Company Limited.) In 1932, Johnnie Walker 'Swing' was introduced. It was uniquely packaged to appeal to transatlantic travellers and the North American market, with a curved base to the bottle that enabled it to 'swing' with a ship's movement and avoid toppling. On each crossing of the luxury transatlantic liners, over 2,500 bottles of Swing were consumed.

During the 1930s the company's progress continued, with a massive expansion of the facilities at Kilmarnock, and in 1933 Johnnie Walker was granted a Royal Warrant as Scotch Whisky Distillers to King George V, an honour that has been renewed by each subsequent monarch.

Shortly after the Second World War, Johnnie Walker Red Label emerged as the world's leading whisky brand, and by 1955 sales had increased fivefold. As Johnnie Walker's enormous export business had

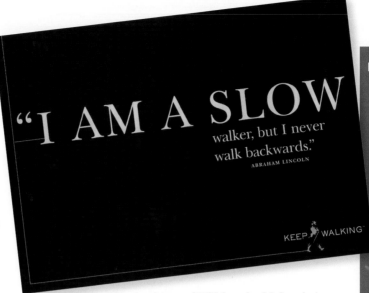

An advertisement of 2001 from the global marketing campaign introduced in 1999 and called 'Keep Walking'.

brought in essential foreign currency to the war-weakened British economy, it was no surprise when in 1966 Johnnie Walker was one of the first winners of the Queen's Award for Export Achievement.

Although the famous Striding Man trademark has been used ever since it was introduced, over the years it has been modified, such as in 1999 as part of a £100 million global marketing campaign called 'Keep Walking'. Then the figure, which has always been seen walking from right to left on the bottle labels, was made to walk from left to right. This was because the marketing men decided that the figure looked as if he was walking backwards into the past and by changing his direction he, and the whisky, were striding towards a bright future in the new millennium.

Johnnie Walker Scotch whisky (Red, Black, Gold and Blue Labels) is now blended and bottled by Diageo in Leven in Fife and Shieldhall in Glasgow. Production in Kilmarnock ended in 2012. As the world's best-selling Scotch whisky is Johnnie Walker Red Label, the Walker name is certainly still 'going strong'.

Information and illustrations courtesy of Diageo

DID YOU KNOW?

Alexander Walker began using the famous square bottle to reduce breakages and made sure much more of his whisky arrived intact at its destination.

By 1920, Johnnie Walker whisky was sold in 120 countries.

In 2012, a limited edition Diamond Jubilee decanter was released with a price tag of £100,000.

There is a bottle of Johnnie Walker valued at $22,577.44. It's a blend of 45- to 70-year-old whiskies, created in celebration of the company's legacy. It is 'generally not for sale.'

Johnnie Walker Swing is supplied in a distinctive bottle whose irregular bottom allows it to rock back and forth, a design originally used aboard sailing ships.

EVE and the ORANGE

Breakey

An alluring advertisement from the 1920s that conjures up the idea of Eve in the Garden of Eden with tempting oranges rather than an apple. However, the bitter taste of a Seville orange, which makes them so suitable for marmalade, would have come as an unpleasant surprise.

If Woman gave Man the Apple, she made up for it afterwards by giving him the orange. It was a Miss Keiller, a lady of Dundee, who invented the original Dundee Marmalade. In the hundred years that have passed since then, who can count the happiness she has brought through her famous confection? Thus woman accomplishes her usual destiny — to destroy one Paradise and make another.

KEILLER'S
DUNDEE
MARMALADE

Famous for Quality for over 100 years

Famous for Quality for over 100 years

14

KEILLER

There is a much repeated story that husband and wife James and Janet Keiller of Dundee invented marmalade.

It goes like this. Towards the end of the eighteenth century a storm-wrecked Spanish ship carrying a cargo of Seville oranges made its way into Dundee harbour. Grocer James Keiller purchased the entire cargo of oranges, but on discovering how bitter they were, he gave them to his wife, Janet, who then invented marmalade, and she and James set up a factory to produce it.

Repeated the story may be, but it is untrue (and Janet was his mother!). Marmalade had been around for a long time before Janet was said to have invented it, and although its source has been lost over the centuries, the term *marmalade* first appeared in the English language as far back as 1480.

James was the youngest son of Janet and John Keiller, a tailor. At the age of twenty-two he joined his mother in her confectionery shop on the south side of Dundee's Seagate. According to the history of Keiller's of Dundee by W. H. Mathew, James was a young man who had made 'some remarkable success in experiments with oranges'. It was he, therefore, not his mother, who produced a novel type of marmalade, based on slicing the peel and making a jelly consistency.

After James's death, at the age of sixty-three in 1839, his widow, Margaret, and her eldest son,

Alexander, took charge of the business, and in 1840 a new shop in Castle Street was bought as well as work premises off the High Street. At that time the business was still mainly that of a confectioner but by 1850, when Alexander took control following his mother's death, marmalade-making, made

Advertisement and stoneware jar from the end of the 19th century.

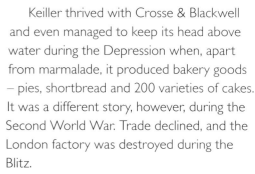

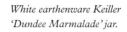

easier with the introduction of peel-chopping machines and steam power, had increased and by 1867 it was the company's main product.

Alexander ran the company for twenty-seven years during which it ranked way above Cadbury and Rowantree. Around 1857, he opened a factory on the Channel Island of Guernsey to evade the high import duties on sugar imposed in mainland Britain.

On Alexander's death, his son John, aged 26, took over the company, and began expanding it. He remodelled the Dundee factory, using the latest technology, and enhanced the confectionery business with a range of sweets including traditional lozenges, gums and rock.

In 1888, by which time the sugar duties had been removed, the company switched production from Guernsey to a new factory at Silvertown in London, to meet the demand for Keiller's products in England and to provide a base for expansion into the export market. To this end, John Keiller travelled throughout Europe, the United States and the British colonies of Australia and New Zealand.

John Keiller controlled the company directly from 1877 to 1893 when it was converted into a limited liability company with John as chairman. Because of ill health, however, he gradually withdrew from the running of the by then hugely successful business, with a range of marmalade, jellies and jams as well as comfits, jujubes, candied peels and bottled fruits. John Keiller died in 1899, aged 49. He was the last of the Keillers to be actively involved in the business, which in 1919 merged with two English-based firms, Crosse & Blackwell and Lazenby's, with Crosse & Blackwell taking complete control in 1922.

Keiller thrived with Crosse & Blackwell and even managed to keep its head above water during the Depression when, apart from marmalade, it produced bakery goods – pies, shortbread and 200 varieties of cakes. It was a different story, however, during the Second World War. Trade declined, and the London factory was destroyed during the Blitz.

After the war, confidence returned, and Keiller modernised their Albert Square factory and built a new preserves factory at Maryfield in Dundee, which during the 1950s was extremely busy producing – as well as marmalade – lemon curd, jams, fruit squashes, cordials, mincemeat and plum puddings.

The start of the 1960s brought a new owner for Keiller when the Nestlé group took over Crosse and Blackwell. It also saw the boiled sweet production at the Albert Square factory increase eightfold. Despite this, however, in 1971 the factory was closed. Meanwhile, Maryfield continued to produce marmalade, and by 1979 sales had doubled.

During the 1980s, changes of ownership of Keiller came fast and furious. Nestlé sold out to the Okhai group, which sold out to Barker & Dobson, which sold its 'Keiller Preserves' subsidiary to Rank Hovis McDougall.

The final nail in the coffin of the Keiller empire in Dundee came in 1992 when confectioners Alma Holdings, which had bought Barker & Dobson, went into receivership. The factory at Maryfield, where sweets such as Keiller's famous Butterscotch were produced, closed. After 195 years, the name of James Keiller & Son was no longer part of Dundee's manufacturing scene.

Today Keiller's marmalade is manufactured in New York by the Hain Celestial Group. It is not shipped to the UK.

15

Lees' famous Macaroon Bar is firmly rooted in Scottish culture. It is one of Scotland's most popular products, requested by expatriates around the world from Canada to Australia.

The delicious treat was invented by accident in 1931 when John Justice Lees, a grocer's son from Coatbridge, was trying to produce a smooth chocolate fondant bar in the premises above his father's shop in Newland Street. The result was a disaster, but as an experiment, John covered the bar in coconut and inadvertently discovered a titbit that would become a Scottish staple – the Macaroon Bar.

Other products, such as tablet, mint ice and snowballs, joined the Macaroon Bar, and by the 1950s sweet-toothed Scots could not get enough of Lees'

confectionery, with Macaroon Bars becoming almost as popular on the football terraces as the half-time pies, both of which were washed down with Bovril.

Lees' products were manufactured in unusual premises, the old Garden Cinema, which had been acquired by John Justice Lees. It was just 200 yards along the street from his father's shop. The stalls were the production area, the balcony the storeroom where the aisles, rows and seating numbers were ingeniously incorporated into a stock-keeping system – for example, Macaroon Bar labels might be found

*A selection of Lees' products
in the early 1970s.*

in row six, seat seven, except the seat was not there. The projection room was another storeroom, and the marble-stepped former ticket booths were shops where misshaped confectionery was sold.

Lees' realised the power of marketing, and for their Macaroon Bars the company came up with one of the best-loved and best-remembered jingles, which was recognised everywhere. Generations grew up with Lees' catchy advertising song and many can still sing it now. It went as follows:

*'Lees', Lees', more if you please,
All of us beg on our bended knees,
For mums and dads and grandpapas,
It's Lees' for luscious Macaroon Bars.'*

Originally, there was a line about 'A tasty treat for picanninnies and grandpapas', which was swiftly changed when a subsequent generation objected to the turn of phrase.

During the 1960s and 70s Lees' continued to flourish, but by the end of the1980s the glory days had come to an end and Lees' empire was crumbling. The company was still a family concern, but John Justice Lees had grown old and so had the factory. In March 1991, the company showed a loss of just under £2 million and the family was forced to sell it to Northumbrian Fine Foods. This was only a temporary reprieve, however, as despite a range of new confectionery products and the development of Heather Cameron Meringues, by Christmas 1992 the company was heading for liquidation and the workers were not sure if the factory would be open when they returned after the holiday.

Fortunately, the New Year brought salvation in the form of Raymond Miquel, the former chairman of Bell's

Whisky, who took control in early 1993 and returned Lees' to independent Scottish ownership. Miquel and his Danish partner, Klaus Perch-Nielsen, own over 50 per cent of Lees' equity. Other investors have 35 per cent, and 10 per cent is held by the Bank of Scotland.

Miquel, who had first arrived in Glasgow from the Channel Islands during the Second World War, had an enviable record of accomplishment. Working his way up from the shop floor, he transformed Bell's from a small distillery into a worldwide brand. On arrival at Lees' he said it reminded him very much of the situation Bell's had been in – it was a brand that everyone in Scotland knew, loved and bought, but it had not tapped into its potential abroad and its facilities were dreadful. It did have potential, however, and it did have the Macaroon Bar.

Within a year Miquel had returned the company to profitability, and by 1998 had moved it to a £4.7million custom-built factory less than half a mile away from the site of the now demolished cinema and the other Heather Cameron factory.

Lees' marked the tenth anniversary of its rescue from bankruptcy by acquiring another Scottish family-owned firm, Waverley Bakery Ltd, which can trace its roots back to 1908 when the Zaccerdelli and Cervi families founded Waverley Biscuits in Edinburgh. As Scotland's only cone and wafer manufacturer, Waverley's products were complementary to Lees' products. The cone is the most environmentally friendly form of packing for ice cream, and its traditional name, 'Pokey Hat', originated from *ecco un poco* (Italian for 'try a little'), the phrase used by Italian ice-cream street vendors when peddling their wares. Wafers first appeared in Europe around the 1660s.

Apart from producing its renowned Macaroon Bars, Snowballs and Teacakes, Lees' is the UK's biggest manufacturer of meringues. It produces over 200,000 meringues nests per day and has 85 per cent of all retail sales. Newer products are Snowcakes, Jaffa Delights and a Dennis the Menace Bar. Lees' struck a licensing deal with D. C. Thomson to use *The Beano*'s Dennis the Menace character on a Coconut Ice Bar, Lees' first product aimed specifically at children.

Originally, Miquel had wanted to license Oor Wullie, another of Thomson's best-loved creations, but Thomson stuck to its long-standing policy of not licensing either Oor Wullie or the Broons.

With its products available from corner shops to major multiples, Lees' has again established itself as a nation's favourite. It also exports worldwide, with even the King of Tonga being a fan of its Macaroon Bars, having been introduced to them by expatriate Scots.

Things look good for the future, so, as the jingle goes: 'Lees', Lees', more if you please'.

Illustrations courtesy of Lees'

The ever popular Lees' Snowballs.

Showcard c. 1935
Every Dog Has Its Day.

56

16

Lyle's Golden Syrup has been named by the Guinness Book of Records as Britain's oldest brand. Its story began in the 1860s when Abram Lyle III became involved with the Glebe Sugar Refinery in Greenock.

Lyle was born in 1820 in Greenock, and worked as a cooper (barrel maker) in his father's business, before starting a small shipping business. He had been transporting sugar for years, when, as payment of a debt, he took a part-share in a local sugar refinery. Discovering that the sugar cane refining process produced a syrup that normally went to waste, he decided to experiment with this by-product and discovered a process that produced a delicious sweet spread and sweetener for cooking.

Wanting a purely family business, Abram sold his shares in the Glebe Refinery and sent his sons Abram IV and Charles Lyle, who had been managing the Glebe Refinery, to London to look for a site for the family's own refinery.

A simple, but impactful advertisement from the 1950's that focuses solely on the product and the brand. The highly recognisable tin design has been in existence almost unchanged for over 125 years and in 2006 it was recognised by Guinness World Records as having the world's oldest branding and packaging.

Land was bought in Plaistow marshes in Silvertown, and in 1882 the Plaistow Sugar Refinery was completed. Many of the workers were brought from Greenock with their families.

In the first year, 1883, the venture made a loss of £30,000, but demand was growing for the golden liquid Lyle stored in wooden casks and sold to his staff and locals, and soon it was being delivered to shops in casks, decanted into dispensers and then poured out into customers' own jars. About a tonne a week was being sold, and a separate part of the refinery was devoted to the product.

In 1885, the product was poured into tins for the first time. The tins were strong, and explorer Captain Scott took some on his ill-fated Antarctic expedition in 1910. When explorers discovered some of the tins in 1956, both the tin and syrup inside it were in good condition.

It was Abram who designed the product's packaging that today is instantly recognisable by 86 per cent of shoppers. He was a religious man, which is why the Lyle's Golden Syrup trademark depicts a quotation from the Bible. The Old Testament Book of Judges, Chapter 14, tells the story of Samson slaying the lion and later finding a swarm of bees forming a comb of honey in the carcass. Samson made this the subject of a riddle: 'Out of the eater came forth meat and out of the strong came forth sweetness'.

Abram decided to have the dead lion and the bees and the second half of the quotation put on all his tins, and in 1904 the lion, bees and quotation were registered as Lyle's trademark. In 1921, the business merged with Tate, a sugar-refining business started by Henry Tate in 1859. The merger produced Tate & Lyle, today the only cane sugar refiner in the UK and the largest in Europe. A rule of the merger, however, was that the Golden Syrup could only be produced at Plaistow.

Nowadays, as well as the classic tin, there is a vast Lyle's Golden Syrup range that includes easy-pour bottles, maple-flavoured syrup, Lyle's Black Treacle and Lyle's Squeezy Syrups. In 2008, a special edition gold anniversary tin was produced to mark that it was 125 years since Lyle's Golden Syrup was first poured into tins – from 1885 to 2008.

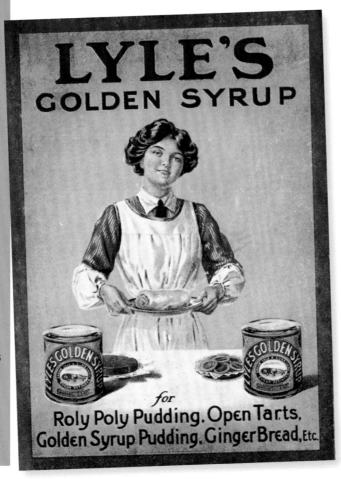

Lady Cooking Showcard c. 1910s.

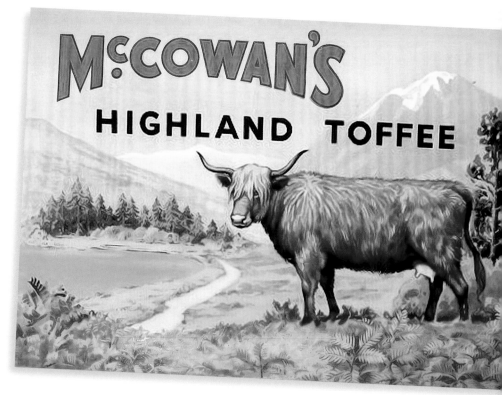

17

Think Highland cow, think McCowan's
Highland Toffee. The two are synonymous,
the Highland cow being the logo of a
product that is fondly remembered by
generations of children and just as much
enjoyed by those of today.

There is much more to the company, however, than Highland Toffee. It also manufactures an assortment of children's confectionery, and while the original Highland cow logo still appears on the Highland Toffee packaging, an updated version has been adopted as the general company logo.

McCowan's Limited has been manufacturing confectionery for almost eighty years. Its founder, Andrew McCowan, was born in Perthshire in the late-nineteenth century. He began work as a herdboy on local farms, little thinking that the Highland cows with which he worked would have such a profound influence on the rest of his life. At the age of seventeen he came down to the Lowlands to seek his fortune, and it was while working as a lemonade delivery boy that his flair for business first emerged. Not content with his wage, he became an agent for a small confectionery firm, selling sweets to the shops to which he already delivered lemonade. He quickly saw that money could be made in the rapidly expanding confectionery market, and in 1905 opened a small 'sweetie' shop in Church Street, Stenhousemuir. A year later, he started wholesaling confectionery.

Shortly before the First World War Andrew branched into manufacturing confectionery in an old store, where the first McCowan's products – different flavours of tablet – were handmade over a coke-fuelled brazier. By 1920, production included rock, snowballs, lollipops and macaroons, and the first motor van had been purchased. By 1922, the company had expanded so rapidly that new premises at the current location in Tryst Road were required.

During the Depression, Andrew recognised the potential for a product offering nutritional goodness at a reasonable price. What he came up with was McCowan's Highland Toffee, and the company's oldest established product was born. This was quickly followed by the chocolate-coated bar and the famous Toffee Dainty, a mouth-sized chew designed for those with lower spending power. Flavouring was the next obvious progression, with the introduction of the Highland Mint Toffee. By the early 1930s, the Highland Toffee lines had become so popular that all resources were concentrated on them.

During the next decade, sales, distribution and the product range were all expanded, and the firm became an important source of employment for the community of Stenhousemuir.

Andrew McCowan died in 1951, and in

McCowan's Highland Toffee with the famous Highland cow logo on the packaging.

*McCowan's Wham and
Vimto children's chew bars.*

1959 his son, Robert, sold the company to Crosse & Blackwell who were in turn brought out by the Nestlé Company in 1960. The business, however, maintained its essential character, continuing to operate as an individual unit under the McCowan name whilst profiting from the technical marketing management and expertise of the international parent company. In 1989, Nestlé sold the company to a management buyout team.

In 1982, McCowan's entered the children's chew market with Wham, a space-age fruit-flavour and sherbet chew bar. Following the success of Wham, the company concentrated on producing innovative products for the children's confectionery market. In 2011 the brand was sold to Tangerine Confectionery, who discontinued McCowan's Highland Toffee. However, the innovative Wham bars are still going strong, produced in Blackpool by Barratt, still in the same retro-wrapper and with the same fizzy bits to make the tongue tingle.

Information and illustrations by courtesy of McCowan's

An advertisement from the 1930's depicting a bonny young child in a warm domestic glow enjoying what else but a McVities and Price biscuit or two.

18

Selection of McVitie & Price biscuits for Christmas 1950.

Biscuits are big business in the sweet-toothed UK, and McVitie's is Britain's leading biscuit manufacturer. As a brand, it evokes trust.

Customers know they can rely on McVitie's to provide a wide range of excellent-quality delicious biscuits that appeal to all ages. Mention digestive biscuits and it is almost 100 per cent certain that the name McVitie's will be mentioned before any other, even abroad, as the brand maintains a No.1 sales position in over ninety locations across the world, including Hong Kong and Scandinavia.

Robert McVitie, born in 1809 in Dumfries, founded McVitie's. He had served an apprenticeship with a Scottish baker before joining his father in 1830 in setting up a provisions business at 150 Rose Street, Edinburgh, a tenement house owned by his father. Three moves later Robert was in 5 Charlotte Place (now Randolph Place), which is where he laid the foundations of a famous Edinburgh firm and where he first described himself as a baker and in 1856 as a baker and confectioner.

Robert had four children, and two of them, William and Robert, were apprenticed to their father's bakery and later sent to the Continent to study bakery and to learn French and German. The result was that Robert McVitie was the first to introduce Vienna bread into Scotland and at one time described his business as the 'Boulangerie Française et Viennoise'.

In 1880 Robert senior retired, and in 1884, aged 75, he died, leaving his business to his son Robert, his other son, William, having left baking to become a journalist.

Although Robert was left a flourishing business, he had seen what Continental bakers could do and was itching to emulate and better them, his horizons having been widened. He therefore set out to expand the business, one of his first steps being to get a bigger bakery and then to appoint Alexander Ross as manager.

Colourful and creative Homewheat advertisement of 1979.

In 1887, a person who was to bring dynamism into the business was appointed – Alexander Grant. In 1892 he developed the first 'Digestive' biscuit as a food to aid the digestive system because of its high content of baking soda, known to help control flatulence, hence the name.

In 1888, Charles Price joined the firm as a salesman on the understanding that if his sales justified it he would be made a partner. His sales did, he became a partner, and the company became McVitie & Price. Price left in 1901 to become Liberal Member of Parliament for Central Edinburgh.

In 1891, salesman George Andrews Brown began to develop the brand in London and the southern counties. He had to persuade the London shops that McVitie's biscuits were better than those of the English biscuit-makers. When he told those in Edinburgh that the 'large Scotch biscuits' were of 'little use in London and that the North's favourite Rich Tea biscuits broke badly', they promptly set out to produce a smaller Rich Tea biscuit to suit the London market.

Although in 1894 the Edinburgh factory burned down, the rebuilding brought benefits with the new works being the most up-to-date in the UK, capable of producing a ton of biscuits per oven per day – a fantastic output at the time. To keep up with the rapidly increasing sales in London, a factory in Harlesden, North London, was opened in 1901.

Robert McVitie died in 1910 at the age of fifty-six. As he was childless, he had made arrangements for the firm to become a limited liability company with Alexander Grant as general manager. In recognition of his great services to the firm, Grant received 5,000 £1 shares, a large sum then.

After facing death in 1915 when he had double pneumonia – then a killer – Alexander Grant realised that to protect his family, a son and two daughters, he

Advertisement for McVitie's tangy Jaffa Cakes.

had to get into a position where he could grow the company ever faster and further. He therefore went to the National Bank of Scotland for backing to buy control of the company. This was forthcoming when the general manager examined the books and saw how successfully Grant was running the company. By 1916, negotiations were complete and Alexander Grant was McVitie & Price.

Alexander Grant died on 21 May 1937. He had been created Sir Alexander in 1924 and had made himself a wealthy and much honoured man by his lifelong application to work. In telling the story of McVitie's, much of it is Alexander Grant's story.

Alexander's son, Sir Robert McVitie Grant, inherited the business. Named in affection for his father's friend and colleague, he had learned the job from the shop floor upwards and in the early 1920s created the popular MacVita as an alternative to Scandinavian ryebread. During the Depression before the Second World War, Robert had managed to install the most modern gas-fired ovens in the industry, putting McVitie in the lead.

Sir Robert died in 1947. He was only 52, and although his early death did not give him much scope, during his time two significant things happened. The first was the rationalisation of production, reducing the 370 varieties of biscuits and cakes produced in 1939 to ten by 1945. The second was starting negotiations leading to the union with Macfarlane Lang & Co., in Glasgow, and the formation of United Biscuits.

The Second World War, with its restrictions on supplies and transport, had seen a successful cooperation under the Cake and Biscuit Manufacturers War Time Alliance between Macfarlane Lang & Co. and McVitie & Price. To continue this and to help realise part of the family interests in the two firms, made inevitable by the burden of taxation and death duties, they formed United Biscuits in 1948.

After the formation of United Biscuits under the chairmanship of Peter MacDonald, McVitie's legal adviser since the 1930s, both Macfarlane Lang & Co. and McVitie & Price retained their separate identities and competed against each other, McVitie developing market dominance. It was not until 1965 that the operations of the two companies were integrated into a single company with Hector Laing, son-in-law of Alexander Grant, as managing director. By 1965, two other Scottish bakeries had joined United Biscuits – Crawfords and Macdonalds.

After the formation of United Biscuits, McVitie & Price, or McVitie's as the brand is now known, steadily increased its share of the market and although new products have been introduced, Digestive and Homewheat Chocolate Digestive have remained as the core products.

Because of the longevity of the brand, its reputation for quality and its ability to keep up with contemporary consumer trends, McVitie's is sure to delight the palates of biscuit-lovers for many more years.

® *Bandit, Crawford's Go Ahead!, Hobnobs, Homewheat, MacVita, McVitie's, Jaffa Cakes, Munchmallow, Penguin, Taxi and YoYo, are registered trademarks of United Biscuits (UK) Limited and used by consent*

120ml

MACKIE'S
of Scotland

HONEYCOMB

LUXURY DAIRY ICE CREAM

*made with molten honeycomb chips,
fresh milk and cream*

120ml

MACKIE'S
of Scotland

CHOCOLATE

LUXURY DAIRY ICE CREAM

*made with chocolate flakes,
fresh milk and cream*

120ml

MACKIE'S
of Scotland

STRAWBERRY

LUXURY DAIRY ICE CREAM

*made with real strawberries,
fresh milk and cream*

19

MACKIE'S
of Scotland

While Mackie's ice cream is the brand leader in the luxury ice cream market in Scotland as well as having an increasing market share in England, British visitors to South Korea must be surprised to find ice cream café parlours going by the name of Mackie's.

This exciting venture began with a London store visit by Kyung Wood Kim, Director of M & B Korea Co Ltd, when he selected Mackie's Traditional Ice Cream as his favourite from the full available range of UK ice creams.

Shipping to Seoul began in 2002 with the supply of ice cream for the Korean World Cup games. Each shipment has to spend about 36 days at sea on a journey of over 11,000 nautical miles, followed by a final train journey to Seoul, with the temperature tracked throughout the voyage.

Korea has the highest population density in the world, and with 50 per cent of the population living in the Seoul metropolitan area, there is a well-established market for ice cream in which Mackie's aim is to become one of the country's top three ice cream brands.

M & B Korea Co Ltd has been rebranded as Mackie's of Asia, and their intention is to expand by franchise in South Korea and from there throughout Asia and possibly Japan.

Back home, Mackie's of Scotland is a family business, and since the start of the twentieth century, four generations have farmed at Westertown Farm near Inverurie in the North East of Scotland.

In 1986, the direction of the business changed, with a shift from traditional farming and milk retail into ice cream production, a transition completed in 1993 when the family converted the traditional byre and old mill into a modern ice cream dairy that can produce over 10 million litres of ice cream each year. A New Product Development kitchen was also created.

Although the most popular product in Mackie's range is 'Traditional', a smooth, creamy ice cream with no added flavours, new products, such as Strawberry and Raspberry Dairy Sorbets and Mango and Orange Iced Fruit Smoothies, have also won excellence and innovation awards.

The farming activity covers 1600 acres of land, and the herd of 500 Jersey and Holstein milking cows are the main focus of the farm, utilising most of the land on which is grown 600 acres of grass and 900 acres of cereal, the bulk of which is processed into feed for the cattle in Europe. The process from milking to ice cream can be completed in less than 24 hours.

Managing the environment is important to Mackie's, who have planted 120 acres of deciduous trees around the farm for beauty and to provide wildlife habitats.

Environmental corridors, a wetland area and pond have also been created to protect and encourage as diverse a wildlife population as possible. The company commitment to the environment is displayed by three 750kW wind turbines which generate all the electricity required for the business – with enough surplus to power about 1000 domestic homes. Mackie's ice cream is made with renewable energy, and in 2008 a lighter, more easily-recyclable packaging was launched.

In 2007, Mackie's was the regional winner for Europe, Middle East and Africa, of the Financial Times Environmental Awards, and the company's vision is to be 'a global brand from the greenest company in Britain created by people having fun'.

Infomation and illustrations courtesy of Mackie's

A Mackie's Ice Cream Parlour in Seoul.

Front page of the booklet 'Nursery Rhymes Up To Date' issued by Marshalls in the 1930s.

20

Marshalls is the leading pasta brand in Scotland. It is produced and marketed by Pasta Foods Ltd, a world leader in the production and marketing of 'snack pellets' and the UK's leading dry pasta producer.

The traditional Marshalls brand, however, has been part of the Scottish menu for generations as it goes back to 1878 when James Marshall, the pioneer of pre-packed refined wheat-based foodstuffs, set up the Ibrox Flour Mills in Glasgow's south side.

Marshall was born in Rothesay, in 1838, and moved to Glasgow in his early twenties to work in W. & W. Glen's flour mill in Cheapside Street. Although he became a partner in Glen's in 1865, Marshall

wanted to work for himself and established his own flour mill producing farinaceous substances known as 'Marshalls' Preparations of Wheat'. Testimony by the medical profession and analyses by chemists that these preparations 'contained all the elements necessary for the sustenance and growth of the human frame' gained them the confidence of the public.

Marshalls' first branded product was Semolina, which contained all the elements of the wheat grain without

Advertisement of 1893 for Farola.

the inclusion of any crude or indigestible products. Cheaper than bread, it was just as nutritious. Marshalls' Semolina was introduced in 1885, and although James Marshall was not the first to manufacture it, his was different in that it was pre-packed, the first such product to become available on the market and an innovation that gained his company a lasting reputation. In the same year, Marshalls' products were protected by the trademark 'The Heart of the Wheat' and James's brother, Thomas, an engineer and an active food reformer, became a partner in the business.

Together, James and Thomas launched Marshalls' second branded product, Farola, a very fine-grained semolina advertised as 'pleasing to the most fastidious and easily digested by the most delicate'. It was marketed as having many uses: mixed with fruit to make blancmanges and other 'ornamental table dishes', as an infant food, an invalid food and as a health food.

The partnership between the Marshall brothers did not last for long. High marketing costs and an over-ambitious level of production forced it into liquidation in 1887. There then followed an acrimonious dispute between the brothers that led to the business being reconstructed into two companies, James continuing at the Ibrox Mill and Thomas setting up in Morrison Street. There was war as each brother battled to capture the market. Thomas claimed to have retained the old firm's trademark, 'The Heart of the Wheat', and warned customers that 'without it none are genuine'. Under the mark he sold semolina and oat flour. On the other hand, James retained the old firm's brand names and advertised himself as sole proprietor of Semolina and Farola.

Although some of the problems of direct competition were eased with the closure of his brother's firm in 1894, following his death the previous year, it was imperative for James Marshall to keep his company's name to the forefront. This he did by advertising extensively in newspapers and magazines and on billboards. He also came to an agreement with bakers Macfarlane Lang (for whom his son, James P. Marshall, was a bakery manager) allowing them to use the trademarks Granola and Farola for biscuits based on the products. Later, Marshall sold Macfarlane Lang the sole right to the title Granola and, in exchange, Macfarlane Lang gave Marshalls the right to use Farola for biscuits.

In 1900, James Marshall converted his firm into a private limited company with the shares distributed among his family. James Marshall and his son, James, still employed by Macfarlane Lang, were the only directors until 1906 when two of James' other sons, Thomas and Allan, joined the board. Three years later, his fourth son, Edward, became a director at the age of eighteen.

While the company survived the First World War, Allan Marshall was killed, a great blow to his father who was eighty at the time. From 1919 onwards James Marshall became increasingly blind, and in 1926 he suffered a further tragedy when his son Thomas died from pneumonia.

During the 1920s, with James Marshall still at the helm (he found it hard to delegate), the company continued to increase sales by creative advertising. It missed very few trade fairs and exhibitions, undertook market research, produced recipe books and provided

Advertisement of 1946 featuring Marshalls' three branded products – Farola, Macaroni and Semolina. Their Scottishness was emphasised by framing the picture with tartan. The wording of the advert shows that supplies were available only in limited quantities because of the Second World War.

a variety of special offers such as calendars and tea trays.

On 28 May, 1928, James Marshall died of heart failure. He had been dedicated to the business and, apart from taking a short break when his son Thomas died, he played an active role until the day before his death.

In 1935, the company introduced the third of its famous branded products, Marshalls' Macaroni. Manufacturers had pursued the idea of producing pasta products before the war but had failed because of difficulties in perfecting the drying process. These had been overcome by the late 1920s and a variety of pasta products, largely unknown to the British table, were introduced.

Over the decades since, James Marshall has expanded into making just about every kind of pasta imaginable, and although the company's ownership has changed, the quality of its products has not. As in the past, great attention is paid to packaging and today a traditional tartan band across the top of a see-through packet that displays the pasta shapes, distinguishes Marshalls' products from others. The range includes Macaroni, Spaghetti, Lasagne, Tagliatelle and, of course, the company's famous Semolina and Farola, both of which have stood the test of time.

21

Bread is Scotland's healthiest fast food and offers exceptionally good value for money – penny for penny it contains more nutrients than any other food. It can help provide a healthy balanced diet for everyone.

When it comes to which is the most popular kind of bread, however, plain is very much an integral part of the Scottish culture. Ask any Scot what reminds him or her of Scotland and plain bread will be one of the answers. Ask which brand is preferred and it's probable the answer will be Mothers Pride, whose distinctive tartan paper wrapper makes it instantly recognisable on the supermarket shelves.

Part of British Bakeries, Mothers Pride has a bakery in Glasgow, a distribution depot in Motherwell and over 700 employees in Scotland. The bakery in Glasgow produces around a quarter of a million loaves per day, 80,000 of which are plain bread.

Mothers Pride Scottish Plain bread has been around since1958, and until the 1970s plain bread was a bigger-selling loaf than pan bread. (Pan bread is so called because it is baked in a 'pan', or a tin.) Plain bread is sometimes called 'square' bread. Its dimensions are three and a half inches by seven inches, and it used to be baked in batches of two, thus a square. The main difference between a pan loaf and a Scottish Plain loaf is the way the latter is produced. It is not baked in tins but on a travelling sole oven, which is effectively baked on a hot plate and batched across the oven. This gives it a hard crust on the top and bottom and soft crumb on the sides. The product is set off on a travelling wood frame that not only assists in batching of the product but also gives it a slightly woody aroma and taste. To give the product stability, Scottish Plain also uses stronger flour than normal white breads. Mothers Pride Scottish Plain is baked with flour milled in Scotland and has 15 per cent more protein than 'normal' white bread.

Scottish Plain is made by a very traditional process compared to pan bread, which is now highly automated. Plain bread is also baked very slowly for around one and a half hours as opposed to pan bread, which is baked for around twenty minutes. Scottish Plain is wrapped in a wax-paper wrapper, the traditional bread wrapping.

When it comes to making toast, research conducted by Mothers Pride found that consumers felt Scottish Plain toast was far superior to other white breads. It doesn't go soggy when spread with butter or served as beans on toast. It doesn't fall apart when dunked in soup and makes great 'soldiers' for dipping into soft-boiled eggs. Toast is not the only way in which the product is consumed. When it is fresh, consumers will almost binge on it. In addition, a 'jeely piece' is not a true jam sandwich unless it's made with plain bread.

Plain bread is much more popular on the west coast of Scotland. Mothers Pride Scottish Plain is generally not distributed farther south than Newcastle upon Tyne. It does, however, make its way down in small quantities and can sometimes be found in larger Tesco and Co-op stores. Sales in the south tend to be concentrated where there is strong representation of Scottish exiles, such as in Corby, Northamptonshire.

Information and illustrations courtesy of Mothers Pride

HIGHLY SUCCESSFUL IN THE HIGHLANDS

NOW AVAILABLE SOUTH OF THE BORDER

A 1989 promotional card that indicated that Mothers Pride Scottish Square Bread was now available south of the border.

22

For such an old and prominent brand as Parozone, the only information available about its beginnings is that contained in an advertisement of 1931: *A Famous Glasgow Product that Keeps British Homes Clean*

Illustrated by Arthur Ferrier a famous Scottish artist, illustrator and cartoonist, this advertisement from the 1920's shows a family in the whitest of white attire and bedding and, quite amazingly, features a poem about bleach.

Just over forty years ago, in 1891, Dr E. J. Mills, an eminent chemist of the Royal Technical College, Glasgow, made a discovery of more than ordinary interest to housewives.

This was a special secret formula for a powerful but safe household cleanser and bleach, which was to bring Science to the wash-tub, lighten labour in the home and save time in countless daily tasks. This epoch-making discovery revolutionised domestic washing and house cleaning in Scotland and Scottish housewives were quick to welcome a new and valuable friend in Parozone.

Since then, the advance of Parozone has been sure and steady, until now, in 1931, it is used throughout the United Kingdom by all home-proud housewives who esteem purity and cleanliness.

It is pleasing to note that despite this great expansion, Glasgow remains the headquarters of the Parozone Co. Ltd., and the distinctly Scottish character of the firm continues unchanged.

Advertisements for household cleaners in the 1930s had a touch of emotional blackmail about them. Manufacturers linked doing the family wash with upholding family values. Housewives who took a pride in producing bright, clean clothing and clean homes were indicating that they took good care of their families. To have lesser standards was to be guilty of slovenly behaviour and of showing a lack of maternal responsibility. Advertisements also appealed to housewives' economical side by stating that products such as Parozone did away with all boiling and scrubbing, which meant that clothes lasted longer. It is believed that the name 'Parozone' was intended to have connotations of good health and cleanliness, with the two elements of the name, 'par ozone', suggesting a meaning of 'by the sea' – the sea and bleach having a common link in chlorine.

The distinctly Scottish character of the firm mentioned in the 1931 advertisement continued until 1963 when Jeyes acquired the product, at that time a thin solution of sodium hypochlorite bleach sold in glass bottles and used mainly for laundry. With the introduction of thickened bleaches in the 1970s, however, coupled with improved laundry powders becoming available, liquid bleach usage moved away from laundry and the main use became toilet-cleaning.

The Jeyes business was originally founded by John Jeyes who first patented a disinfectant fluid in 1877. Jeyes was granted the Royal Warrant in 1896 and since then has been proud to supply the Royal Household with cleaning solutions. This royal patronage is one of few that have remained in place for over 100 years, during six successive reigns. The company now designs, manufactures and markets household cleaning and freshening products in more than 60 countries and the company currently boasts sales in excess of £200m.

Under the Jeyes banner the Parozone brand became a market leader with many UK firsts. Among them were: perfumed bleach; a 'flip-top' cap with a liftable nozzle, making the bleach easier to direct under the toilet rim; liquid bleach with added limescale deterrent; a 'drop-in' cistern bleach block; flushable toilet surface wipes; and a liquid rim product to deliver bleach and fragrance. In 2001, Parozone pushed its new range of limescale-removing Fizz Tabs and flushable Toilet Wipes in a 2 million pound advertising campaign. The ads featured the toilet-cleaning exploits of a dim-witted man and his cleaning-savvy wife and carried the strapline 'Parozone Does The Job'.

Since 2005, Parozone bleach has a unique patented no spill cap with safety valve. This, Jeyes claimed, is the first product to address consumer fears about the dangers of spillages associated with handling bleach.

In 2013, brand design consultants were brought in to give Parozone bleach a new brand identity and packaging to compete with market leader Domestos. The re-designed packaging displayed the image of a protective shield and placed emphasis on the product's powerful germ-kill ability, communicating to consumers the fact that it can help to protect their precious families from germs, as well as keep their homes clean. The new identity was implemented across liquid bleach, in a range of fragrances.

Glasgow's Dr Mills would be gratified to know that his Parozone lives on, although much removed from his pioneering product.

'You don't know how white, white can be until yoou use Parozone!' Advertisement of 1936.

'Home is Brighter the Parozone Way'. Advertistement of 1952.

P...P...Pick up a...

Penguin became the highest-profile McVitie's sub-brand in 1966 when the P....pick up a penguin' ads first appeared on our TV screens. The slogan became one of the most memorable of the decade.

Penguin biscuit wrapper saying from 1955.

23

Although Penguin chocolate biscuits now come under the McVitie banner, it is such a popular brand that it deserves a mention of its own.

It was not originally a McVitie product. It was created in 1932 by Macdonalds Biscuits, founded in Glasgow by William Macdonald who began his business life as a salesman working for several biscuit manufacturers. He then went out on his own as a food commission agent and as a side-line imported cream-filled wafers from Antwerp, which he sold at less than half the price of similar products on the market.

Next he leased a small factory in Cardonald, Glasgow, and began chocolate-coating biscuits manufactured by others, which was so successful that in 1928 he became a biscuit manufacturer, a cherished ambition and a brave decision, as he was fifty-three years old and had a wife and six children to support.

It is not known why the name 'Penguin' and the symbol of a giant emperor penguin was chosen by William Macdonald and his advertising agents, but whatever the reason the name has become one of the most well-known and popular in the history of chocolate biscuits.

After William Macdonald Biscuits joined United Biscuits in 1964, the brand came under the McVitie banner. (McVitie and Macfarlane Lang had formed United Biscuits in 1948.) Over the years, McVitie's association with the appealing birds, represented in Penguin advertising, has strengthened the brand. The name is regarded as memorable and fun, and has led to such entertaining advertising campaigns as 'P-P-P-Pick up a Penguin', with which McVitie's introduced Penguins on television in 1965, with the actor Derek Nimmo saying the memorable words.

Pick up a Penguin is exactly what President of Russia, Vladimir Putin, did in 1991 when he was a bodyguard for Anatoly Sobchak, Mayor of Leningrad. They were part of a trade delegation to Ford's Bakery in Prestonpans, East Lothian, and were there to close a deal to set up a bakery in Leningrad to train Russian bakers how to make biscuits. Apparently, at the signing ceremony, Putin, having spotted a plate of Penguin biscuits on the table, went over, picked up a handful and stuffed them into a pocket. As he left, everyone could see the biscuits sticking out of his pocket.

'Perfect when you're Peckish'. Along with other chocolate biscuit bars, Penguin benefits from the increasing number of people needing tasty, satisfying biscuits that can be eaten 'on the hoof' or as part of a packed lunch.

Autumn 1995 saw the introduction of the first new Penguin flavour since the original milk chocolate version. It was 'Penguin in the Dark', a darker chocolate biscuit covered with dark chocolate.

McVitie's used a unique recipe with all the taste of dark chocolate without the bitterness associated with it. This successful venture led to the introduction of the Penguin Variety – a multi-pack of milk, plain, orange and mint chocolate biscuit bars.

The start of the twenty-first century saw a relaunch of the brand and new Penguin products such as Splatz – vanilla- or chocolate-flavour cream splatted between two chocolate biscuits. Also new was Chukka – flip-top pots filled with biscuit, chocolate and caramel pieces. Chukka was introduced with a fun TV advertising campaign featuring three Highlanders dressed in kilts and tossing cabers. They run out of cabers and just as they are wondering where to get more, a happy-go lucky penguin

According to this advert from 1952, there was nothing like a Penguin. Covered with creamiest milk chocolate it was only 3 1/2d. for the biggest chocolate treat. Customers were invited to look for the bright red, green or blue foil wrappers when they were shopping. 'Have a Penguin today' it finished.

carrying a fishing rod comes along and says 'Hello, Ladies, seen any wild trout about?' The men look at each other and the penguin becomes a caber and gets 'Chukked'. Penguin is McVitie's most popular chocolate biscuit bar, with sales growing daily.

® Penguin, Splatz and Chukka are registered trademarks of United Biscuits (UK) Limited and used by consent.

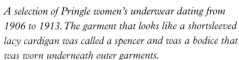
A selection of Pringle women's underwear dating from 1906 to 1913. The garment that looks like a shortsleeved lacy cardigan was called a spencer and was a bodice that was worn underneath outer garments.

24

SCOTLAND

A 1910 men's underwear garment of the style that evolved into outerwear worn by sportsmen.

Pringle, one of the oldest names in the Scottish Borders, the birthplace of Scotland's knitwear industry, was founded in Hawick in 1815 by Robert Pringle. Initially it produced woollen hosiery but by 1827 was manufacturing men's and women's knitted underwear, using the highest-quality wool fibres.

In 1858, Pringle was the first company in Hawick to introduce the steam-driven frame. It was also when Robert's son, Walter, invented intarsia knitting, such as its diamond pattern for which Pringle became famous. Robert died in 1859, and Walter carried on Robert Pringle & Son. In 1878, at the age of sixteen, Walter's son, Robert, joined the company as an apprentice, and later became a partner in the company.

During the last decade of the nineteenth century Pringle was a pioneer in the underwear world. It introduced spun-silk underwear, which became a world-famous brand. On the knitwear side, Argyle-patterned

A selection of women's Pringle knitwear in the early years of the twentieth century; (top) Glen coat and (bottom) a Norfolk jacket both of 1910.

Pringle

The look you love . . . superlative
soft-as-silk cashmeres . . . in
out-of-this-world colours . . . new Pringles
in tune with the trend of fashion.

Left. WESTBURY
Absinthe, paradise blue, ivory
or Bermuda pink
34" - 42" £7. 7. 0.

Right. ARLINGTON
Eau-de-nil, paradise blue,
carnation or butterscotch.
34" - 42" £7. 19. 0.

PRINGLE OF
SCOTLAND LTD.
HAWICK

Late 1950s advertisement showing the Royal Warrant that they acquired in 1956.

socks were introduced and a cable stitch developed by Walter Pringle was used on a range of women's Norfolk coats, Pringle being one of the first firms to introduce knitted outerwear.

The Edwardian age brought a relaxation of manners and style. There was a craze among men and women for active sports such as cycling, tennis, golf and swimming, and there was a need for flexible, informal clothing like the woman's knitted sports coat, a loose, long cardigan, often belted, which came in about 1909 and was widely worn on informal occasions from then on.

Sportswear evolved from underwear that had absorbed sweat and prevented chills after exertion. People would actually turn their clothing inside out, as exemplified in the one-piece bathing suit, basically woollen combinations worn as outerwear. Other switches came when women began wearing their decorative lace-topped spencers (short-sleeved undergarments) on the outside as blouses and men began wearing their undershirts outside, which is when the 'sweater' was born. By 1917, industrially-produced knitwear resembling the sweater as we know it today had become recognised as everyday apparel and was established as an important outerwear garment.

Apart from Robert Pringle & Son becoming a private limited company in 1922 (Walter Pringle's only son had died in the war), the 1920s were unremarkable for the company. The 1930s, however, were a different matter. They were exciting times for Pringle and the fashion trade. Courtiers Chanel, Patou and Lanvin gave knitwear the stamp of importance as sweater blouses and sweater suits became part of their collections twice a year. Schiaparelli launched her fashion career with sweaters and in America colleges, girls adopted the 'sloppy joe' sweater, a long loose-knit garment. The sweater had become a necessity for the modern woman.

In 1934, Austrian designer Otto Weisz was hired. He brought a new dimension to the Border knitwear trade with his sensitivity to market nuances and his appreciation of the importance of styling and colour. He was responsible for the first 'styled' collection in 1934. However, it was when he created the 'twinset', a sweater and a cardigan of the same colour worn together, that Pringle became the industry's pacesetter.

In 1955, a menswear division was opened with the introduction of the Ryder Cup golf shirt. Two years later, Pringle clothed the British Ryder Cup Team. The Ryder Cup golf shirt was Pringle's first sortie into golf clothing, later largely responsible for the decline of the company.

The 1960s saw the discontinuation of underwear production after 134 years, golfer Arnold Palmer representing Pringle's golf clothing, the appointment of the first woman designer and the takeover of the company by Dawson International in 1967.

Under the leadership of Dawson, Pringle floundered. When twinsets went out of fashion in the 1970s, the company relied on golfing sweaters and in 1981 began a sponsorship deal with golfer Nick Faldo. Initially this went well, but the brand became dated and instead of being synonymous with high fashion, as in the past, it became synonymous with Argyle-patterned jumpers worn only by golfers and middle-aged men.

With its continued reliance on the Faldo sponsorship deal, by 2000 the brand was practically bankrupt, which is when Kenneth Fang of S. C. Fang & Sons, a worldwide knitwear manufacturer based in Hong Kong, bought it. He then returned Pringle to private ownership and hired Kim Winser, previously the only female director of Marks & Spencer, as chief executive. When she took over, the first thing to go was Faldo's £1.5 million a year sponsorship deal. As Kim realised that she had an amazing brand with

Model Sophie Dahl wearing a classic knitted cardigan with co-ordinating pink knickerbocker-style trousers. Sophie was chosen as the face of Pringle when the brand was re-launched in 2001. This advertisement was one of a series featuring Sophie labelled as 'Miss Argyle'.

a wonderful heritage and the potential to become great again, she employed visionaries rather than manufacturing experts who knew how to run a plant.

Pringle Scotland was relaunched as an international fashion brand in 2001. Although the mission was to revamp the brand's image, its Scottish heritage was retained, with the famous Argyle pattern finding its way on to some of the garments.

An amazing bit of luck for Pringle came when David Beckham purchased four of their sweaters and wore one of them at a book-signing session. Victoria Beckham was then seen wearing a Pringle jacket. More unsolicited publicity came when celebrities such as Pierce Brosnan, Madonna, Claudia Schiffer, Jamie Oliver and Robbie Williams were seen wearing Pringle garments.

When Pringle made a loss of £9 million in 2007, Fang embarked on a global restructuring, leading to the closure in 2008 of the plant in Hawick that had been in operation for almost 200 years. As the head office in Scotland was retained, the company was accused of only keeping it on so that it could continue to use the successful brand name Pringle of Scotland.

Information and illustrations courtesy of Pringle

DID YOU KNOW?

Although Pringle Scotland is an internationally renowned quality fashion brand, for over a hundred years underwear was its mainstay.

In 1908, Pringle developed a formula for unshrinkable underwear and guaranteed that all wool-and-silk and wool goods, stamped with the trademark 'The "Rodono" Finish' that did shrink in washing, would be replaced.

British cinema stars of the 1940s such as Jean Simmons, Margaret Lockwood and Deborah Kerr endorsed and advertised Pringle knitwear. They were the 'sweater girls' of their day.

In April 1955, a pink Pringle cashmere twinset appeared on an *American Vogue* cover.

An important product in the Robertsons range since 1891, their Golden Shred Mincemeat has been a kitchen cupboard staple on Christmas shopping lists ever since.

25

Robertson's is famous for the fine quality of its preserves and especially for its first product, 'Golden Shred' marmalade, whose origin goes back to 1864.

Four famous Robertson labels – Golden Shred, Bramble Seedless, Silver Shred and Mincemeat. This advertisement dates from the 1960s at which time all these products were being manufactured in Paisley.

Born in 1832, the founder of the company, James Robertson, started his working life in a thread mill in Paisley. There was a recession in the industry, however, and as his future seemed insecure and he wished to become a shopkeeper, he left the mill, took a cut in salary and began an apprenticeship in 1847 with Messrs. Gibson and Craig, wine, spirit and tea merchants at 107–8 High Street. Being ambitious, during his apprenticeship he attended night school classes at Seedhill School, where he was taught reading, writing and arithmetic.

When he was twenty-seven, James Robertson achieved his ambition to have his own grocery shop.

Little did he know, however, on that day in 1859 as he stood outside his premises at 86 Causeyside that he was destined to make the world's finest preserves.

Despite being shrewd in business, James was a kind, charitable man, and one day in 1864 he took pity on a struggling salesman and agreed to purchase a barrel of bitter oranges from him, even although he knew they would not sell well. He was right – sales of the oranges were very slow, and it would have ruined the tiny business if they could not be disposed of quickly. The solution came from his wife, Marion. Rather than see the oranges go to waste, she suggested that she should make them into marmalade to be sold in the shop.

'A Breakfast Favourite the World Over'. A clever and colourful 1950s' advertisement for Golden Shred that shows the Robertson Golly seated at a table set on top of the world, which is shown as a giant orange with eyes, a nose and a mouth. When the Golden Shred drips from Golly's spoon, the orange's tongue sticks out to catch it. The slogan 'Robertson's Golden Shred Puts the Taste on the Toast' appeared on all advertisements.

Marion's tangy marmalade, clear with orange shreds throughout, was an immediate success and, realising the full business potential his enterprising wife had uncovered, James set about perfecting her recipe and somehow found a way to remove the bitterness of the orange while still retaining what he called 'the highly tonic value of the fruit'. This was the secret of the delicious Robertson's flavour and is the same secret that, even today, gives all Robertson's preserves their special flavour.

Marion Robertson is credited with coining the name 'Golden Shred', which James registered as his trademark for the clear type of marmalade, for which the business became famous. She came up with the name as she held a jar of marmalade up to the window and was taken by the golden light filtering through the orange jelly and shreds of orange. The product was so popular that in 1864 a separate company was formed to lease a factory on Stevenson Street to meet increased demand. Later, a lemon marmalade named 'Silver Shred' was introduced, as well as jams and products such as 'Golden Shred' Mincemeat.

With sales soon covering the whole of Britain and countries abroad, additional factories were opened: the famous jam works at Droylsden, near Manchester, in 1890; Catford, London, in 1900; and Brislington, Bristol, in 1914. There was also a plant in Boston, USA. So well thought of were Robertson's products that in 1907, Shackleton's Antarctic Expedition included Golden Shred in its supplies.

Until recently, Robertson's trademark was their famous 'Golly', which first appeared in 1910 when one of James Robertson's sons, John, brought a Golly doll back from the USA and put its picture on the Robertson's price list. Soon afterwards the Golly symbol, with his red trousers, yellow waistcoat and blue, long-tailed jacket, was incorporated into every product label bearing the Robertson name.

Jolly Golly badges have featured famous golfers, cricketers, footballers, musicians and the Golly Lollipop Man, which appeared on all Robertson's road-safety materials produced for schoolchildren. The Golly badge scheme was the longest-running collector scheme in Britain. Over the years only minor changes, such as the positioning of the eyes and the smoothing of the hair, were made to the Robertson Golly, now replaced by the more politically correct Paddington Bear.

Many fruits are used in the manufacture of Robertson's products – bitter or Seville oranges, lemons, redcurrants, blackcurrants, apricots, apples, plums, blackberries or 'brambles', raspberries, pineapples and damsons, which take their name from Damascus and have been cultivated in that area of the Middle East since before the Christian era. The use of 'bitter' or 'Seville' oranges in marmalade dates from the reign of Henry VII.

The Paisley factory closed in 1979, and after a couple of takeovers Robertson's became part of Premier Foods, who sold it to the Hain Celestial Group

In 2010 Robertson's adopted Paddington Bear to adorn their Golden Shred label, as he is famous for his love of marmalade sandwiches. He always carries a jar of it in his suitcase and usually has a marmalade sandwich tucked under his hat – 'in case of emergencies'.

in 2012. Today, Robertson's products are manufactured in Histon, near Cambridge, by Hain Daniels. The Royal Warrant presented to Robertson's by King George V in 1933 continues as a testament to the continued quality and popularity of Robertson's Golden Shred.

DID YOU KNOW?

In 2001, the Golly collectables were replaced by Roald Dahl-created characters illustrated by Quentin Blake. These included the BFG, Matilda, James from *James and the Giant Peach* and Willy Wonka.

Robertson's officially 'retired' Golly in 2002, insisting that they did this for commercial reasons rather than political correctness.

Robertson's jam disappeared in 2008 when owner Premier Foods decided to focus solely on its ever-popular Golden Shred Marmalade.

Since 2014, Paddington Bear has adorned Robertson's Golden Shred jars, in a sponsorship deal to coincide with the film of the same name, and its sequel.

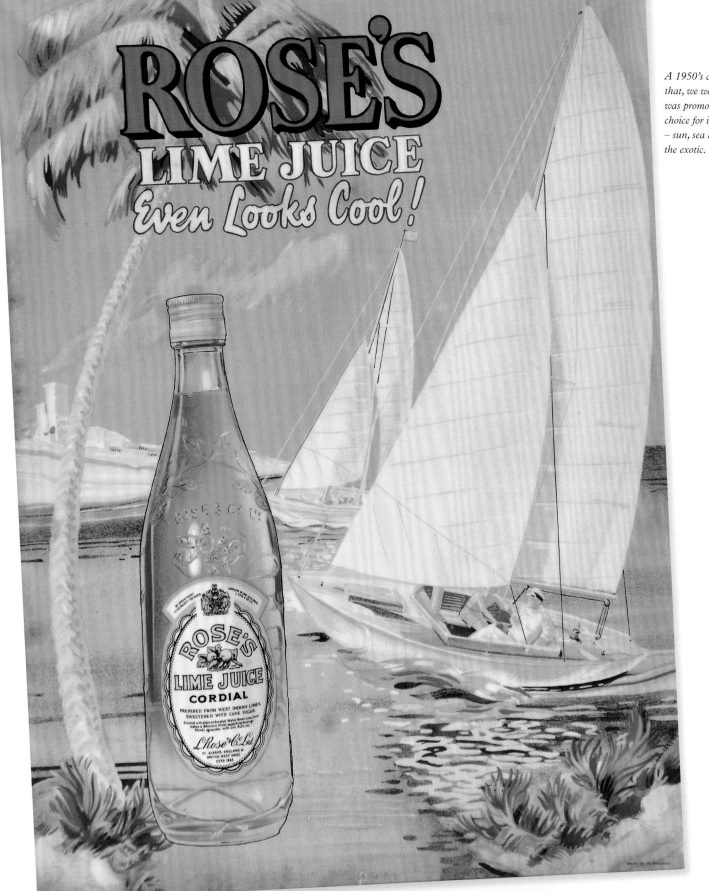

A 1950's advertisement that, we would now say, was promoting a life style choice for its consumers – sun, sea and sand and the exotic.

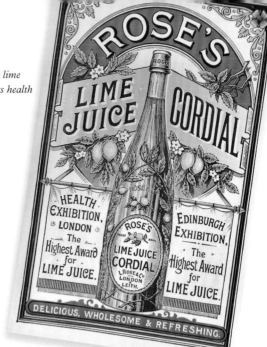

An early label for the lime juice that promoted its health giving properties.

26

Scotland gave the world its first concentrated bottled fruit drink – Rose's Lime Juice Cordial. It was the invention of Lachlan Rose, a member of a Leith family business of ship repairers and chandlery supplies.

Lachlan, a younger son, had started up a second business in 1865 to provide food supplies to ships leaving Leith. It was called L. Rose and Company and specialised as lime and lemon juice merchants.

The reason behind the formation of the new company was that, from 1795, it had been customary for ships of both the Merchant Marine and the Royal Navy to carry a supply of lime or lemon juice when on a long voyage to counteract the effects of scurvy. It was an Edinburgh doctor, James Lind, who discovered that a diet including citrus fruits was the most effective way of preventing scurvy, and when Captain Cook adopted the new treatment during his great

expeditions of the 1770s, he lost only one man to scurvy in three years.

Because lime juice kept better than the juice of the other citrus juices that also contained vitamin C, the Merchant Shipping Act of 1867 made it compulsory for all British sailors on long sea voyages to be given a daily ration of lime juice to prevent scurvy, hence the sailors' nickname, 'Limeys'.

The year 1867 was also when Lachlan Rose patented the process for preserving lime juice without the addition of alcohol. Until then it was supplied to sailors laced with 15 per cent rum as a preserving agent. He had discovered that the preservative, sulphur dioxide, would prevent the juice from fermenting. He realised also that by adding sugar to his product and putting it in eye-catching bottles, he could market it to a wider public. Thus Rose's Lime Juice Cordial, the first branded fruit juice, was born.

L. Rose and Company went from strength to strength, 'furnishing delicious, cooling and refreshing beverages eminently suitable for family use'.

The limes for Rose's Lime Juice were grown on the island of Dominica in the West Indies, and to ensure a regular supply, in 1893 the company purchased its own

estate on the island. It also developed plantations of lime trees in what is now Ghana, in West Africa. Today, the limes come from Peru or Mexico.

While the company started in Leith, in 1875 it transferred its headquarters to London and then in 1940 moved to St Albans to avoid the Blitz. When it moved to St Albans, it also opened a depot at Boxmoor, which is on the Grand Union Canal near Hemel Hempstead. Ships carrying concentrated lime juice would dock in the Port of London and, for convenience, the barrels of juice were loaded directly on to barges that travelled up the Thames and the Grand Union Canal to be unloaded at Boxmoor. As lime juice is no longer brought into the Port of London and the factory at St Albans has closed, barges are no longer required.

The secret of Rose's Lime Juice's unique flavour is a combination of the maturity of the fruit (seven years), the speed with which it is crushed – as soon as it falls off the trees – and the crushing process itself. After the limes are selected, they are washed in clear running water and then crushed between giant granite rollers in a mill.

Rose's is now owned by the C&C Group, headquartered in Dublin.

Advertisement of 1947 for Rose's Lime Juice, which indicates that supplies were unavailable even two years after the end of the Second World War. Although their products were unavailable, to keep them alive in the public's mind companies continued to advertise them. This advertisement makes a point about the weather when the man says to the doctor, 'But I like my temperature. It's the first time I've been warm for months.' The year 1947 was one of the coldest on record, with freezing temperatures for months.

27

Advertisement for Tennent's Bombay Export Pale Ale.

It is likely that anyone going for a pint in Glasgow will order a Tennent's lager, manufactured in the company's massive brewery in Duke Street, Glasgow.

Tennent, as the city's oldest commercial business, is steeped in history, the Tennent family's connection with brewing going back to 1556 when Robert Tennent was a private brewer and maltser.

Until the beginning of the nineteenth century, ale, or 'yill' as it was known, was the staple drink of the Scots. Private maltmen brewed it on a small scale and delivered it round the houses. Families of standing and innkeepers brewed their own. Gradually, private brewing died out and public breweries appeared, one

of these being H. & R. Tennent, founded in 1740 by brothers Hugh and Robert Tennent in rented premises in the Drygate area of Glasgow. Apart from it being a traditional area for brewing, as it was there that the monks had once brewed their ale, the reason the Drygate was so popular with brewers and maltsers was because of its close proximity to the Molindinar Burn, which provided a vital ingredient – water.

H. & R. Tennent's new brewery, however, had no need of the Molindinar, for it had its own supply of fresh,

clear water from a deep well within their property. It also had its own maltings and barley from the family farm of Easter Common (now the Petershill area of Glasgow).

H. & R. Tennent flourished, and it is recorded in city records that at Christmas 1745, on their way back from Derby, Prince Charles Edward Stuart and his bedraggled Jacobite army stopped at the brewery for sustenance. There they received ale and 'each and every man was refreshed and heartened by the brew'.

By the end of the eighteenth century the company's name had changed to J & R Tennent, the Drygate property had been bought, plus five acres of the adjacent Well Park lands, and an export trade had been established with large consignments of beer and stout going from the Clyde to North and South America.

The Victorian era was the most significant in the history of Tennent. By the 1850s, it had a large general business, a specialist trade in pale ales and stouts, and was the largest exporter of bottled beer in the world. In the 1860s, it began using what is probably Scotland's best-known brand symbol, the Tennent red 'T' trademark, registered in 1876 for sole use throughout the British Empire, as the firm had large colonial sales as well as in the home market. In 1885, Hugh Tennent, aged twenty-two, introduced the drink that revolutionised a nation's drinking habits – lager. Hugh suffered from tuberculosis and frequently convalesced in Europe. During a trip to Bavaria, he sampled the

Advert of 1889 for J & R Tennent's pilsner lager beer stating that it was superior to anything imported. The new lager brewery had not been completed at the time.

new light-coloured German beers that were threatening Tennent's Pale Ale market and decided that J & R Tennent should produce a similar product.

When Hugh returned home, his idea was laughed at. There was no way, everybody thought, that such a beer would be popular in Scotland.

Nevertheless, Hugh was determined and in May 1885 the firm began brewing lager in a small way, using its existing plant. The experiment was successful. Scotland took to the pale, sparkling light drink, and in 1889, Hugh commissioned a complete German lager brewery to be built alongside the existing ale brewery. To ensure its success, German brewer Jacob Klinger, who had been a consultant when lager brewing began, was put in charge of the venture, which a Glasgow newspaper condemned as 'a madman's dream'. Klinger chose engineering German contractor L. A. Reidinger of Ausburg, who had set up plants in places like Yokohama and Buenos Aires, to create Tennent's German-style brewery, built entirely on a German model, even German coopers being imported to manufacture the cellar casks required for maturation.

The lager brewery was completed in 1891, but Hugh Tennent did not live to see his ambitious project become reality. He died in 1890, aged twenty-seven, and was the last member of the family to be in direct control of the company. His belief in a Scottish lager was justified, however, as in the 1890s, as well as the company winning many important awards, a German lager brewer described Tennent's lager as the best he had ever tasted.

The introduction of Tennent's lager ensured worldwide recognition for the Tennent brand, its reputation eventually rivalling that of its famous German, Danish and Dutch competitors.

Although throughout the years the lager has undergone many transformations, the brew drunk today is based on the original recipe. What has changed, though, is the way it is made. Today, production is by up-to-date technology; then, it relied on manual labour with one group of workers giving rise to a derogatory Glaswegian expression. They were the women employed to clean the massive oak casks in which the lager was matured. Logically, they were known as 'scrubbers', a term that over the years became associated with women who could, at best, be described as a little rough.

When it comes to containers for its products, Tennent has always been in the forefront. By the end of the nineteenth century, it had its own pottery for the manufacture of the stoneware bottles, then required for its products. It then went on to green or amber glass bottles, and in 1936 it was a pioneer of the 'beer can' when it introduced its cone-topped, crown-capped cans, affectionately known as 'Brasso' cans because of their similarity to a can of Brasso metal polish. Tennent's early beer cans were sold only to ships' stores.

The 'Brasso' can, typical design of the time. Carried on the reverse was an assurance that the 'can opens like a bottle and pours like a bottle', and that it 'cools quickly and takes up less space in the refrigerator or ice box'.

A show card of the late 1950s showing a delectable young lady and the two-glass can, which has hardly changed since its introduction in 1955.

The 'Brasso' cans were phased out after the Second World War, and in 1954 an American-style flat-topped can was introduced for the export market. A year later, Tennent introduced the 'two-glass' sixteen-ounce can for the domestic market. 1959 to 1961 brought the Scottish Series (scenic views). 1962 brought the 'English Series' and 1964 saw the launch of the 'Housewives' Choice', twenty model girls, allegedly housewives, each accompanied by a recipe using beer.

Launched in January 1965, initially on the export market only, was the 'Ann Series', featuring Tennent's first can girl, model Ann Johansen, in various situations – at the pool, in the garden, sunbathing, boating on Loch Lomond. It was not the first time Ann had appeared on a Tennent can. She was the girl in the orange dress in the picture of Trafalgar Square from the 'English Series'. She was also one of the 'Housewives'. A second series, 'Ann's Day' – twelve scenes from a model's typical day – and a third, more risqué, series, 'Ann on Vacation', never appeared on the home market. The response to these series from men stationed overseas was phenomenal and up until 1969 Ann featured on every can of lager and export sold by Tennents, and on every can of lager and stout until 1974 and 1980 respectively.

In 1969, the best-known advertising campaign in the

history of canned beer, Tennent's famous 'Lager Lovelies', replaced Ann on the lager cans. For the export market, they were called Tennent's Girls. The original Lovelies were Linda, Pat, Angela, Susan and Vicky. Among subsequent Lovelies were beauty queens Marie Kirkwood and Lorraine Davidson, both of whom had held the Miss Scotland title. In 1982, all the current Lovelies appeared in the 300 poses that made up the 'Can Girl Calendar', obtained by sending in twelve special ring-pulls. The offer was open for less than three months during which 30,000 calendars were requested.

Prominent though they were, the Lager Lovelies were just part of an integrated advertising campaign for Tennent's products, involving billboards, press and award-winning TV advertising, such as the brash, exuberant, catchy 'Tennent's Special' commercials.

Although no more, the Lager Lovelies are not forgotten, as their cans are in the hands of collectors worldwide and are avidly sought after.

At the beginning of 2003, Tennent Caledonian Breweries was voted Glasgow's favourite business, a great boost for the brand and the people who work in the establishment. Tennent is owned by the Belgian brewing giant Interbrew, the second largest brewer in the world.

Information and illustrations courtesy of Tennent

One of the cans from the series 'Ann on Vacation', confined to the export market as the pictures were considered too risqué for the home market.

Poster c. 1930s advertising The Royal Bank's foreign exchange services.

28

RBS
The Royal Bank of Scotland Group

While The Royal Bank of Scotland received its royal charter of Incorporation on 31 May 1727, its beginnings lie in the Act of Union in 1707, when England agreed to pay Scotland a pecuniary 'Equivalent' of £398,085 10s. sterling in compensation for the disastrous Darien expedition and other losses and bets arising from the Union.

In addition, Scotland was to receive a proportion of the increase in tax revenue expected to result from the Union – the 'Arising Equivalent' as it was called. When the Equivalent arrived in Edinburgh, however, only £100,000 instead of the expected £400,000 was in coin, and it was only after protest that another £50,000 was sent from London. As £150,000 was insufficient to compensate all the creditors in coin, many had to be satisfied with debentures – the government's promise to pay at some future date with interest.

An early Royal Bank ledger that includes the entry for the first cash credit, granted to William Hogg Junior. Resting on the ledger are pocket scales used to check the weight of coins that might have been filed or clipped. Also shown are notes and coins of the time, including The Royal Banks' guinea note and an 'option clause' note.

Two societies of debenture holders were formed, one in London and one in Edinburgh, but both were wound up in 1724 when the Equivalent Company, registered in Scotland, was created. Soon the directors of the new company wished to extend its rudimentary banking services beyond the membership of the defunct societies. They wanted to look after other people's money as well as their own. They wanted the company to become a bank.

Consequently, the Equivalent Company applied for a charter in banking in Scotland only. South of the border, the Bank of England held an unbreakable monopoly, but in Scotland, the Bank of Scotland's twenty-one years of monopoly had expired in 1716 and had not been renewed. The name 'Equivalent' was dropped, and a charter incorporating The Royal Bank of Scotland was granted on 31 May 1727, under the great seal of Scotland.

The Royal Bank of Scotland opened for business on 8 December 1727 at the foot of Ship Close in Edinburgh. It had a capital of £111,347 and authority to 'exercise the rights and powers of banking' in Scotland. As extra capital, the new bank called up £22,000 from its subscribers as a banking fund. It also gained control of £20,000, representing the belated payment under the Act of Union, whereby the government was required to pay that amount to Scotland to be lent out at interest for the improvement of fisheries and general manufacturing. Opportunely, the whole sum was deposited with The Royal Bank as the chairman and the majority of the trustees and commissioners of the board had been Equivalent proprietors. The old bank, the Bank of Scotland, had expected to receive half of it on interest.

Immediately the new bank embarked on a ruthless and vigorous campaign to destroy the Bank of Scotland (established in 1695) by the collection and presentation of large quantities of its notes, and by May 1728 the

two banks were frostily negotiating a possible merger. Unable to agree to merge, however, the two banks resigned themselves to an uneasy coexistence.

Instead of establishing branches, The Royal Bank developed connections with the growing number of provincial banking companies, thereby pioneering correspondent banking in Scotland. Without branches, however, the expansion of its note issue proved difficult, and a new approach was adopted. The Royal Bank's links with Glasgow, where it had been closely involved in financing the tobacco trade, had been strong from the outset, and in 1783 it opened a branch in a small shop at Hopkirk's Land, near Glasgow Cross. The timing was right, for the Glasgow banks had lost much of their drive and invested much of their funds in government loans.

Robert Scott Moncrieff and David Dale, appointed joint Glasgow agents, established a huge business in the discount of bills of exchange, thereby altering the entire balance of the bank's affairs and accounting for at least half its business. The Glasgow branch of The Royal Bank moved into the Stirling Mansion in Queen Street and when, during the radical uproar of 1820, there were fears that the mob would plunder the bank, Captain Smith's Guard of Sharpshooters was quartered there for more than a week with triple sentries at the gates. As the bank held much of the city's valuable plate and treasure, it was regarded as 'The Mint' or 'The Tower' of Glasgow.

In 1819, the bank's headquarters moved from Edinburgh's congested Old town to St Andrew Square in the New Town, occupying from 1825 a magnificent townhouse built in 1772 for Sir Lawrence Dundas of Kerse, then Governor of The Royal Bank. This building is still the bank's registered office.

During the early years of the nineteenth century, it became clear that the restriction of the bank's note issue to Edinburgh and Glasgow would curtail the future growth of the business, and by 1836 six branches had been opened in Dundee, Rothesay, Dalkeith, Greenock, Port Glasgow and Leith. After the collapse of the Western Bank in 1857 The Royal acquired a number of its agencies and in 1864 the Dundee Banking Co. was acquired.

In 1874, authorised by a private Act of Parliament, The Royal Bank followed the example of other Scottish banks by opening a branch in London. Four years later, the disastrous collapse of the City of Glasgow Bank left the Scottish banking world shaken. The manager, secretary and six directors of the City of Glasgow Bank were arrested on a charge of fraud, tried and jailed.

A positive result of the disaster, however, was the adoption by all the banks of the practice of having their accounts and balance sheets audited by professional independent accountants. Despite difficult trading conditions, during the last years of the nineteenth century The Royal Bank continued to thrive, and by 1910 it had 158 branches and around 900 employees.

The declaration of war with Germany on 4 August 1914 brought uncertainty to banking. A royal proclamation extended the bank holiday period for three days, and a moratorium was declared under which the obligation of the banks to pay their depositors was temporarily suspended. The banks were drawn into funding the government's war loans and advances, and note issue increased rapidly. As small denomination notes were in great demand, special Treasury notes of £1 and ten shillings were issued. Scottish bank notes, where £1 notes were the norm, were declared legal tender both north and south of the border for the duration of hostilities.

After the war, The Royal Bank embarked upon a policy of expansion in London, acquiring Drummonds Bank in 1924, Williams Deacon's Bank in 1930 and the

Engraving of c.1820s of The Royal Bank's registered office, Dundas House in St Andrew Square, Edinburgh. The house was build in 1772 for Sir Lawrence Dundas of Kerse, then Governor of The Royal Bank. Sir Lawrence died in 1781, and thirteen years later the house was sold to the government and became the principal office of Excise in Scotland. In 1825 the Crown sold the house to The Royal Bank of Scotland which, in the 1850s, added the magnificent rear domed banking hall (left). The coat of arms in the pediment dates from when the house was the excise office and is the royal coat of arms of George III. It remains on the building because of a ruling by the Lord Lyon that it is a right belonging to the property rather than to the institution that occupies it.

Introduced by the National Bank of Scotland, Britain's first mobile bank gets its first customer, a representative from the Harris Tweed Association.

old London Bank of Glyn, Mills & Co. In 1939 when war was imminent.

Expansion continued during the 1950s and 60s, with the opening of new branches in Scotland and London and the launch of new services such as personal loans and cash dispensers. By 1968 economic pressures led to further consolidation, and in 1969 The Royal Bank of Scotland merged with the National Commercial Bank of Scotland. After the merger, the new Royal Bank, with 693 branches, enjoyed over 40 per cent of Scotland's banking business.

In 1985, following the failure of rival bids to acquire The Royal Bank of Scotland Group by the Standard Chartered Bank and the Hong Kong and Shanghai Banking Corporation, The Royal Bank merged the businesses of Williams & Glyn's Bank and The Royal Bank of Scotland. The result of the merger was that both banks traded together throughout Britain as a single entity – The Royal Bank of Scotland plc. .

The 1990s brought a refocusing on The Royal Bank's core business of retail banking by selling off its merchant bank interests and acquiring, in 1992, the Edinburgh-based private bank of Adam & Company. In 1994 it launched Direct Banking. In 1997 it announced the UK's first fully fledged online banking service over the Internet, the setting up of Royal Bank Direct Loans, a telephone-based personal lending service and launched joint financial services ventures with Tesco and Virgin Direct.

In 2000, The Royal Bank of Scotland Group acquired National Westminster Bank plc. in a £21 billion deal, the largest takeover in British banking history.

While at the time the acquisition of the National Westminster Bank was the largest takeover ever seen in British banking history, it was nothing compared to that of October 2007, when The Royal Bank of Scotland Group paid £49.1 billion for its Dutch rival ABN Amro, making it the world's biggest banking takeover. Unfortunately the bank paid too much for ABN Amro, and as the takeover took place in 2009, just as the banking boom was about to turn to bust, it led to the group suffering the biggest loss in British corporate history of £24 billion. On 1 December 2008, the Government became a 57.9 per cent shareholder in the group. When shareholders snubbed a £15 billion share offer to shore up its capital buffer, the Treasury handed over a cheque for £20 billion.

Although it is the world's fifth largest bank, The Royal Bank of Scotland Group remembers its roots by maintaining a tradition of innovation and service that began in 1728, with the bank's invention of the overdraft.

29

Est. 1890

Tunnock's is one of Scotland best-known brands. Each week the company turns out millions of biscuits that are sold in tens of thousands of shops around the world.

The business today, however, is far removed from its modest beginnings. Born in 1865 to a well-known Uddingston family, the founder of the company, Thomas (Tom) Tunnock, began an apprenticeship in Aberdour Bakery in Uddingston's Old Mill Road, the same place where the Tunnock factory is today. By working hard and saving some of his earnings, in 1890 Tom was able to pay £80 for a small shop and bakery, with contents, at Lorne Place in Bellshill Road, Uddingston.

The sign above Tom's shop read 'Thomas Tunnock, Purveyor', signifying that he would provide food and services for all kinds of special occasions whether it be for a bridal banquet or a celebration high tea.

Trade flourished as Tom purveyed weddings, christening parties, soirees, picnics and excursions, with each person being provided with a good selection of freshly baked savoury and sweet things. Motivated by his success, Tom opened a tearoom in the same road as his bakery, and, never one to miss an opportunity, he advertised it for hire as: 'Commercial Dining Room for Socials, Smokers and Presentations. Ladies' Accommodation'.

Despite Tom's early success, in the years before the First World War business was so low that the bakery could not support the whole family, leaving Tom with no option but to ask his son, Archie, to find other employment rather than work in the baker's shop.

Archie bought a Ford and an Argyle car and started a car-hire firm, beginning a lifelong interest in the car trade. Archie's business, however, was short-lived. War was declared in 1914, and in 1916 he sold his two cars and joined the Army. He was sent to Iraq where he remained for three and a half years without leave.

Trying to keep the company going during the war took its toll on Tom's health, and in 1919 the bakery

Archie Tunnock's new, larger tearoom in Uddingston Main Street, which he opened in 1924 and which remains today with its original shop front.

had to be closed down. A year later he died, at the age of fifty-four.

Although Archie had not planned to become involved in the family business, he knew he had no choice but to help his mother re-open the derelict bakery, which contained only a single hotplate and an old hand-operated dough divider. After buying a bag of flour, 28 pounds of lard and a hundred eggs, however, Archie began baking morning rolls, small Paris buns and doughnuts, simple items that he knew how to prepare. His mother helped in the shop, 'holding on to the till'. Later he re-employed one of his father's bakers, Michael Scott, who spent the rest of his working life with the firm.

Archie followed his father's tradition of purveying for local functions. Burns' suppers, Christmas and New Year parties, picnics and excursions were all grist to his mill.

Although several bakeries were put out of business during the Second World War, Tunnock's was lucky. Cakes and buns were still baked as the company had generous allocations for essential ingredients. There always seemed to be a queue outside Tunnock's shops.

It was, however, in the 1950s that the business really expanded and produced the products for which it was to become famous. Archie realised that there was more to the business than catering. What he wanted was to come up with a product that no one else made, a speciality item. He therefore decided to experiment and bought a dozen dry wafers from an Italian shop and with the help of a man who knew how to boil toffee, found he could combine the wafers with caramel. The result was the world-famous Tunnock's Caramel Wafer, launched in 1951 and made to a secret recipe that defies imitation.

Archie had brought his sons, Tom and Boyd, into the business, and Tom was responsible for overseeing the Caramel Wafer process from beginning to end.

Piping hot caramel being poured in the Tunnock's factory.

The Caramel Wafer was only the beginning of the products that made a fortune for the company and the Tunnock family. After it came Snowballs, soft mallow covered by chocolate and coconut. Following Snowballs was the Caramel Log, and in 1956 Tea Cakes, soft mallow encased in a delicate chocolate shell on a biscuit base.

While Archie Tunnock created all the new products, their success was a joint effort between father and sons. It was Archie, however, who realised the importance of having the right packaging. While at first he sent out wafers and mallows in plain cardboard boxes, he discovered that for one penny more he could have gaily coloured containers with cut-out lids that folded into attractive display stands. 'That bit of colour,' he said, 'almost doubled my sales overnight.'

Archie Tunnock continued to take a close interest in the business until his death in 1981 at the age of eighty-six.

By then both his sons, Tom and Boyd, were running the company. Tom died in 1992, and Boyd is now in charge of the company, helped by his daughters, Karen and Fiona, the fourth generation of Tunnocks to be involved with the company.

Boyd Tunnock received an MBE in recognition of export achievements. 'It stands for My Biscuits are Enjoyable,' he joked. While he would be the first to say that his company's products are the best, Boyd has been known to confess that he loves KitKats. Like his father and grandfather, he puts in long hours and for relaxation sails his yacht *Lemarac* ('Caramel' backwards). Enough said.

As well as its famous products, the factory, which employs around 600 townspeople, produces a full range of traditional Scottish products for the Tunnock tearoom in Uddingston and is still famous for its wedding cakes.

Every year, offers to buy the company arrive, and the Tunnock family could stop working immediately. All approaches are rejected, which speaks volumes.

Information and illustrations courtesy of Tunnocks

DID YOU KNOW?

During the Second World War a specialty of Tunnock's was trifle, topped with synthetic cream unaffected by rationing. The trifles were made by the thousands, packed in boxes and delivered by tramcar to shops all over the west of Scotland.

The Caramel Wafer is a worldwide household name, and each week well over three million are exported to more than thirty countries, including Saudi Arabia, Japan, the United States, Canada, Trinidad and the West Indies. One of the firm's secrets is that, however hot the climate, none of the chocolate sticks to the wrapper.

For the export market the biscuit was marketed as 'Piper' Caramel Wafers, with a picture of a Scottish bagpipe player on the wrapper.

A Highlander and proud of it

An advertisement of 1973 for Walkers Highlander Shortbread which was a more rugged type of shortbread – thicker, more crunchy and rolled in demerara sugar.

The cake that's a 'dram' come true. Walkers' rich fruit cake, which has Glenfiddich single malt whisky added to the mix.

PRODUCT OF SCOTLAND

Walkers
– ESTABLISHED 1898 –

Glenfiddich Highland Whisky Cake

Glenfiddich
HIGHLAND
WHISKY CAKE

Walkers

THE CAKE THAT'S A DRAM COME TRUE

Made with all Walkers' traditional baking craft, together with generous amounts of Glenfiddich malt whisky, this rich and delicious highland Fruit Cake is sure to become the toast of your customers.

The Glenfiddich Whisky Cake has all the flavour of the Highlands - outside and in. It is presented in a distinctive re-usable tin featuring paintings of Scottish scenery depicting all the life

and legend of the spectacular area that is home to both the world's finest shortbread and to the most famous malt whisky producer.

Baked using only the finest ingredients, the Glenfiddich Whisky cake gives a taste of all that's best of the Highlands and will be sought after as a luxurious and prestigious gift.

30

PRODUCT OF SCOTLAND

Walkers

·— ESTABLISHED 1898 ·—

While some Scottish companies play down their 'Scottishness' when trying to capture international markets, this is not so for Walkers of Aberlour, which exports 45 per cent of its products.

Walkers' shortbread gift tins in their distinctive red tartan bearing classic romantic paintings from Scotland's historic past capture the traditions of chivalry and rebellion that shaped a nation.

Sold in more than 65 overseas markets, Walkers shortbread is recognised as being the finest in the world and the company proudly proclaims its origins by giving its products a distinctive red tartan packaging and a logo showing a picture of Bonnie Prince Charlie and Flora Macdonald.

Walkers, the largest family-run UK biscuit manufacturer, was established in 1898 by Joseph Walker who, with the help of a £50 loan, opened a village bakery in Torphins, near Banchory in Aberdeenshire. He was only twenty-one and had served an apprenticeship with Mitchell & Muil's bakery in Aberdeen. Joseph had very high standards, and with his mind set on creating the world's finest shortbread,

he spent his first year in business perfecting his recipe. Thanks to the excellence of his products, Joseph's bakery thrived, and in addition to his local year-round customers, those who visited the district during the fishing and shooting seasons would find their way to his shop. The lodges and grand houses, famous for their lavish entertaining when occupied by shooting parties, were also valuable sources of local trade. Demand for Joseph's products grew so rapidly that in 1909 he moved to a larger shop in Aberlour, which still trades today, selling bakery goods.

As the years went by Joseph's business prospered, and after the First World War his two sons, Joseph and James, joined him in the shop.

By the mid-1930s, not only was the day-to-day trade such as bread and biscuits doing well, there was also remarkable demand for shortbread and cakes. Clearly, Walkers insistence on using only the finest flour, butter and other natural commodities in its products had paid off. By the start of the Second World War, shortbread was packaged in tins, making it even more transportable. Unlike the colourful tins of today, however, the first ones were plain with a printed-paper wrapper.

The post-war years saw gradual expansion, and to correct the high labour cost of producing the general baking lines, it was decided in the mid-1950s to concentrate on the production of shortbread, it being less labour-intensive in proportion to the ingredient cost.

Expansion continued, and by the 1960s James Walker's three children, Joseph, James and Marjorie, had entered the company and were taking responsibility for running and developing it. By the end of the 1960s the business was supplying most of Speyside, via its twenty vans and shops in Grantown-on-Spey, Elgin, Aviemore and Aberlour.

As the demand for shortbread had increased dramatically, to take advantage of markets throughout the UK the pure-butter shortbread was given an increased shelf-life by improved watertight packaging that kept the product in perfect condition, preserving the fresh bakery taste for a year. By then the company was supplying such important shops as Harrods and Fortnum & Mason.

Despite the 1970s being economically difficult for Scotland, Walkers continued to expand, with a move to a purpose-built factory at the edge of Aberlour village in 1975.

Overseas sales became so successful that Walkers received the Queen's Award for Export Achievement three times. In 1987, Walkers received the first ever Highland Business Award, granted to the company making the greatest contribution to the economy of the Highlands of Scotland. Recognition also came from Europe with Monde Selection in Geneva awarding Gold Medals for Walkers' products in 1986 and 1989.

Walkers' packaging has come a long way from plain tins with printed-paper wrappers, for today, as well as carrying a distinctive red tartan, it features, among others, a famous painting of Flora MacDonald saying farewell to Bonnie Prince Charlie, the most romantic moment of Scottish history. Since the 1960s, this image has stared out at us from every outlet where Walkers' products are on sale. The Walker family had seen it in a book, liked it and, as it was out of copyright, decided to use it. Although the company was using the painting, however, it did not own it and had no idea who did until, at the beginning of 1998, it received a phone call from Sotheby's in London to say that 'their' painting was up for auction and would Walkers be interested in bidding. It now proudly hangs in the company's boardroom.

Walkers is an outstanding example of what Scotland has to offer. Its story is one of admirable success, brought about by never compromising on quality and by marketing its products superbly. Joseph Walker succeeded in making the world's best shortbread, a tradition being carried on today by his descendants, who own and manage the company.

Illustrations courtesy of Walkers

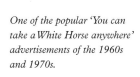

31

The history of White Horse is linked with the island of Islay, off the west coast of Scotland, during the old days of smuggling.

One of the popular 'You can take a White Horse anywhere' advertisements of the 1960s and 1970s.

There, the enterprising Johnstone family operated ten separate 'bothies', little one-room huts in which illicit stills produced *uisge beatha*, the Gaelic for 'the water of life' – whisky. Islay was one of the principal sources of illicit liquor, an illegal trade that flourished until 1816 when John Johnstone combined the ten bothies into a legal distillery called Lagavulin, taken from Gaelic and meaning 'the mills in the hollow'.

The Graham family succeeded the Johnstone family at Lagavulin and joined forces with James Logan Mackie to create the firm of J. L. Mackie & Co. Mackie, a relative of the Grahams, had started his business career in the 1840s with Alexander Graham, a Glasgow spirit merchant and agent for Lagavulin and Laphroaig Distillers in Islay, which were owned by his

brother, Walter. When Alexander Graham retired in 1850, Mackie took over the business, trading under his own name. It was some time later that Mackie joined forces with the Graham family at Lagavulin.

In 1878, a man who became one of the great pioneers and personalities of the Scotch whisky industry joined J. L. Mackie & Co. He was James Mackie's nephew, Peter Jeffrey Mackie, who was sent to learn his craft at Lagavulin where he developed a passionate and lifelong interest in whisky distilling.

Following his training, Peter Mackie developed his uncle's business into one of the world's great whisky firms. He became the senior partner in 1890 and, determined that the firm should start blending, set up a new company, Mackie & Co., for that purpose. The blends, made up in bulk in the company's warehouses, were sold to breweries and spirit merchants in the south of England. Later, J. L. Mackie & Co. and Mackie & Co. were amalgamated to form Mackie & Co (Distillers).

Peter Mackie was the first to recognise the importance of maintaining a continuous standard of whisky and a brand name for it, and in 1890 he registered his own brand, 'Mackie's White Horse Cellar Scotch Whisky'.

An amalgam of Highland history and atmosphere inspired Mackie to choose the name 'White Horse' for his product, the name and the date on the label, 1742, deriving from one of the most famous ancient inns – the White Horse Cellar in the Canongate of Edinburgh, close to the Mackie family home.

Patronised by literary and theatrical notables, the inn served as a favourite off-duty rendezvous for officers of Prince Charles Edward Stuart's Highland Army when it was

One of the successful 'I can tell it blindfold' advertisements of the 1930s.

quartered in Edinburgh during the rebellion of 1745, and was steeped in history. It was from here that the stagecoach to London would set off at five in the morning every Monday and Friday, a journey proudly advertised in February 1745 as taking eight days (God permitting) and granting intrepid travellers the privilege of a fourteen pound luggage allowance.

There is more than one explanation as to how the inn got its name. One is that White Horse Close, which housed the inn, was named after the white palfrey that carried Mary Queen of Scots to and from the nearby Palace of Holyroodhouse. Another is that it was named for a white horse owned by the innkeeper, which won a race on Leith sands, saving its owner from bankruptcy. In gratitude, the innkeeper was said to have kept the horse idle for the rest of its days besides setting up its portrait in his sign.

Whisky was initially sold only in export markets and was not launched on the home market until 1902 where, within five years, it sold 27,000 cases. Sales continued to climb, and by the outbreak of the First World War it was the favourite whisky of countless army messes and had a strong position in both the home and export markets.

As well as producing his own brand of whisky, over the years Peter Mackie acquired distilleries – Lagavulin which the company inherited in 1889; Craigellachie in 1915, which Mackie and a partner built in 1892; and Hazelburn in 1920. At Hazelburn, Mackie set up a laboratory where Masataka Taketsuru learned the craft of whisky distilling that enabled him to set up Suntory and Nikka in Japan.

Known as 'Restless Peter', Peter Mackie was described as 'one third genius, one third megalomaniac, and one third eccentric'. His philosophy was clear: 'As in other things, there are good and bad whiskies. If we cannot afford to buy the best, especially in the matter of Scotch whisky, we should save our money and go without.' He met all cautionary advice with the words 'Nothing is impossible', a term that became a byword within the company. He was a champion of high standards in Scotch whisky and a great fighter for the cause of allowing whiskies to mature. He was a passionate Conservative and an outspoken critic of Lloyd George, then Chancellor of the Exchequer, whom he referred to as 'a Welsh country solicitor' for his attacks on the whisky trade and for the imposition of punishing taxes on Scotch whisky. Lloyd George was teetotal, and during the First World War declared drink to be a deadlier enemy than Germany and Austria. Mackie also ridiculed the Cabinet during the war, accusing them of 'frittering their time in war films and having themselves in cinema shows'. Despite this, Mackie accepted a baronetcy in 1920 from Lloyd George's coalition government.

After Peter Mackie's only son was killed during the First World War, he threw himself into the promotion of White Horse Whisky. He regarded the whole world as his marketplace and travelled it in search of new outlets for the brand, setting up White Horse as a market leader in many countries.

Under Mackie's leadership White Horse achieved an international status that never diminished, establishing great prestige both for the brand and the Scotch whisky industry as a whole. Restless and eccentric he may have been, but a notice in his Glasgow office summed Mackie up – one side said 'Honesty is the best policy', the other said 'Take nothing for granted'.

When Peter Mackie died in 1924 the name of the company was changed to White Horse Distillers, making White Horse Whisky a rare example of a product that later gave its name to its producer. Three years after Mackie's death, the Distillers Company Ltd,

This American advertisement for White Horse appeared in New Yorker magazine in October 1938.

which he had always prevented buying his business, bought it, completing the amalgamation of the Big Five – James Buchanan & Co., John Dewar & Sons, Haig & Co., John Walker & Sons and White Horse Distillers.

The top-rated White Horse, whose key malts in the blend are Glen Elgin and Lagavulin, enjoys an international reputation. It has won many awards for excellence and is shipped to various countries where Scotch whisky drinkers appreciate its distinctive taste. Peter Mackie's legacy lives on in his White Horse Whisky.

Information and illustrations courtesy of Diageo

DID YOU KNOW?

Mackie would hold his annual Peter Mackie's White Horse general meetings at Craigellachie distillery, during which he would forcefully air his opinions on the industry and the British Empire.

White Horse was even available in the United States during Prohibition. Whisky was legally imported into the country as medicine and American doctors prescribed White Horse for medicinal purposes.

During the influenza epidemic following the First World War, green and gold stamps were issued by White Horse bearing the words: Alcohol The Only Remedy for Influenza – Scotch Whisky for Preference. Such advertising is prohibited today, as it is socially irresponsible to link alcohol with medicinal properties.

32

William Younger & Co. owed its beginnings to sixteen-year-old William Younger, who left his home in Linton, Peeblesshire, in 1749 to work as a brewer in Leith.

In 1753 he gave it up to become an exciseman. As his earnings increased, he invested in land, property, a share in a ship, a partnership in a stagecoach company and a brewery. By 1769, however, William was overworked and ill, and on 5 May 1770 he died, aged thirty-seven.

William left his widow, Grizel, £4,270 Scots plus his property and business investments. Of all her husband's business interests, Grizel thought the brewery seemed most likely to provide a living for

her family, so she sold his other enterprises, advertised herself as Mrs Grizel Younger the brewer and took her eldest son, Archibald, on as an apprentice.

The Younger story now moves to William's three sons, Archibald, Richard and William, who all set up brewing businesses. Archibald was the first to do so by starting a brewery in the grounds of the Abbey of Holyroodhouse in 1778. By 1788 he had a new brewery in Croft-an-righ, an ancient lane behind Holyroodhouse, his brother Richard owned a small

Top left: Label for Younger's India Pale Ale bearing the company's triple pyramid trademark introduced in 1859.

Above: Export label for Edinburgh Strong Imperial Ale made for Irving, Macarthur & Co., Demerara, British Guiana, South America.

brewhouse in Gentle's Close, off the Canongate, and William II, the youngest brother, was helping his mother run her Leith brewery.

In 1793, Archibald opened a new brewery in the North Back of Canongate, a move that brought him a fortune, as the new premises were larger, with better facilities and a well of good spring water. In the same year his brother William opened vaults for the sale of ale and porter in Blair Street, Leith. Three years later, William had his own brewery, which, like Archibald's, had been set up within the Abbey's grounds. By 1803

1930s Younger pub signs. The one in the top right-hand corner hung outside Edinburgh's Holyrood pub and that in the bottom left-hand corner hung outside the Coach and Horses in Bruton Street, London, built in the early nineteenth century and given a mock-Tudor façade in the mid-1930s. Amazingly, during the Blitz the buildings on either side of the Coach and Horses were destroyed, leaving the pub intact.

he had bought James Blair's Abbey Brewery in Horse Wynd, which he developed so successfully that he was able to buy a country estate of 600 acres at Beattock, Dumfriesshire.

Richard Younger, who had been quietly brewing in Gentle's Close, left for London to become a partner in the brewing firm of Younger and Ryrie, his sister Jean having married into the Ryrie family. While there he invented, according to the patent, 'a new and improved method of extracting worts from malt, barley and other grains and substances'. Richard died in 1806.

In 1819 Archibald Younger, a bachelor, died, leaving everything to William who, after his mother's death in 1821, consolidated all the family interests under the name of William Younger and Co.. William then set about becoming Edinburgh's foremost brewer. In 1825 he bought an old house in the Canongate, once the town house of the Marquess of Lothian, named the Lothian Hut. Neighbouring ground followed and a building whose adjoining property he had leased with an option to buy in ten years' time. This gave William another small brewery, a coach house, a malt loft, a barn, a kiln, offices, houses and a well. All this was converted into the Abbey Brewery.

The growth in premises brought a commensurate growth in sales, and by 1830 Younger's strong ales were being dispatched throughout Scotland, reaching as far as Shetland and Orkney. The northeast of England was an important market, and even in London, where competition was fierce, the company was well established. By 1840 William was exporting to the USA, Central and South America, most of the British colonies and the West Indies.

When William Younger II died in 1842, as did his partner Alexander Smith, their shares were left to their sons, William III and Andrew Smith, who had been made partners in 1836. During the 1840s, under their direction, trade grew rapidly.

Younger's fortunes during the last four decades of the nineteenth century fluctuated but a new century saw the company's premises still growing and its output amounting to one-fourth of the entire quantity of ale produced in Scotland.

The 1920s began with Younger installing a plant for bottling chilled and carbonated beer, with products such as Sparkling Ale, Holyrood Ale and Scotch Ale making an appearance. These moves, however, coincided with a fall in drink consumption partly because of a revival of the temperance movement, but mostly because of the high cost of a pint thanks to another rise in beer duty. To fight back, brewers improved their public houses and promoted new products. Younger did this by introducing 'Father William', the genial white-bearded old gentleman so long familiar in advertisements for his red waistcoat and yellow check trousers.

In December 1930 came the announcement that Younger and one of its competitors, William McEwan, had 'negotiated a combination of certain of their financial and technical resources with a view to developing the efficiency of the production and

distribution of their ales …' The new partnership, known as Scottish Brewers, officially came into being in 1931 with a subsidiary, McEwan-Younger Ltd, being formed to handle the joint export and naval and military trade of both firms.

The Younger story lost its individuality when it became part of Scottish Brewers, which, when it merged in 1960 with Newcastle Breweries, became Scottish & Newcastle Breweries, which then came under the Heineken UK banner. Younger's is now owned by Marston's, who produce Younger's Special and Younger's Best at their Bedford Brewery.

Information and illustrations courtesy of Scottish & Newcastle

Poster of 1909 showing a British tourist climbing a pyramid to reach a bottle of Younger's Monk Ale. The inspiration for the pyramid theme of the advertisement came from the company's pyramid trademark, prominently displayed.

GONE BUT NOT FORGOTTEN

33

Askit

Askit fights the misery of a backache

Two of the popular and humorous Askit Miseries advertisements which ran from 1971 to 1994.

Although Askit powders are a household name, most people would be surprised to discover that they originated in Glasgow and go back to the early 1900s when Adam Laidlaw and his wife opened a small apothecary's shop in Keppochhill Road, on the north side of the city.

As at the time it was common for customers to ask apothecaries to prescribe cures for lesser ailments such as colds, flu and hangovers, Mr Laidlaw devised an APC (aspirin, phenacetin, caffeine) powder that he sold as an effective relief for headaches, colds, flu, neuralgia, neuritis, arthritis and all nerve pains – in fact, a panacea. He maintained that his proportions plus the use of caffeine citrate (not alkali) and the addition of an antacid, magnesium trisilicate, held the secret of his product's success. Over two years, 300 to 650 powders per week were sold to Mr Laidlaw's customers.

Askit fights the misery of the morning after

Above: An Askit advertisement that appeared in The Bulletin *newspaper of 11 December 1936. The company advertised prolifically in the press as well as on buses, railway station signs, hoardings and theatre curtains and in theatre programmes.*

Right: Askit label of 1939 which stated that Askit was 'absolutely safe', a statement that is not allowed today as advertising restrictions and controls advocate that everything has to be credible, and 'beyond belief' and the old Askit wording implied the incredible.

At the end of the First World War, Mr and Mrs Laidlaw employed a young accountant, John McRobbie Low, to act as their financial adviser. John had returned from the war and had resumed his career with a Glasgow firm of chartered accountants.

Shortly after appointing John Low, Mr Laidlaw felt he was becoming too old to give his product the support it deserved. He therefore asked his young accountant if he would take it and do something with it. As John Low agreed with Mr Laidlaw about the product's potential, his answer was 'yes' and in 1920 a manufacturing company was created. Apart from finding finance, however, there were a couple of other problems to be addressed. One was that, as 600 powders per week was the maximum number that could be weighed and packed by hand, some form of mechanical device would have to be designed to produce the same product in the same pack as before but in far greater quantities at much higher speeds. The second problem was that the product had no specific name. This however, was solved when two young girls wanting to buy an obviously personal item entered the

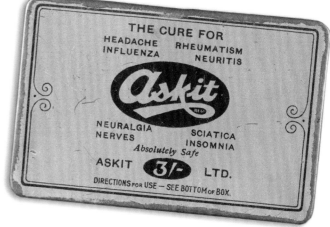

shop with diffidence. One said to the other, 'If it's the lady chemist, I'll ask it, if it's the man chemist you ask it.' In the Glasgow dialect the 'a' is narrow, as in 'arrow', and the word 'for' is omitted. Mrs Laidlaw, who was in the back shop at the time, heard the conversation and immediately felt she had found the perfect name for her husband's analgesic powders – Askit. The next day the name was registered and the Askit Manufacturing Company was born.

Askit Manufacturing moved into a purpose-built building in Saracen Street, Possilpark, in 1920, which was opened by Lord Provost Swan of Glasgow. At this point, those involved in Askit Manufacturing decided to form a limited company and, on 13 April 1925, Askit Limited was incorporated. By the mid-1940s the company was employing around forty workers and producing around twenty million powders a year compared to 20,000 in 1920.

Right from the start, Askit was not shy in advertising. It knew it had a first-class analgesic product that 'cured' headaches, colds, flu and all nerve pains, and it was not afraid to say so. It used all the advertising media available at the time – the press, buses, railway station signs, hoardings and theatre curtains – all of which had the slogan 'Is there an Askit in the house?' Theatre programmes also carried Askit advertisements and 65 per cent of Scottish buses carried the slogan 'Askit, the safe remedy'. All advertisements carried the additional message 'Powders 3d and 1/6d'.

While in Askit's early years all advertising was relatively free from restrictions and controls, in the late 1960s, restrictions were introduced. In Askit's case the phrase 'Relief beyond belief' was rated as unacceptable as statements had to be credible, and 'beyond belief' implied the incredible. Similarly, 'An Askit tonight, tomorrow all right' indicated a speed of action in a medicine that was not allowed. The words 'safe' and 'cures' were banned.

In view of the restrictions, a complete change of Askit advertising had to be found, and as at that time commercial television had come to the fore, it had to be geared to that medium. Askit rose to the occasion and came up with what was one of the most successful and longest-running (1971–1994) campaigns ever – The Askit Miseries

– which revolved around animated drawings by Roger Hargreaves (creator of the *Mr Men* books) of the ailment characters of headache, cold, flu and sore back. The tagline was 'Askit Fights the Miseries'. Audience reaction was immediately strongly in favour and Askit's image was elevated overnight. The campaign was revolutionary for analgesic advertising.

Because visual movement was involved, other media, like bus backs, station signs and hoardings, virtually disappeared, leaving television as the main thrust of any campaign, backed up by press.

The Askit Miseries were replaced by an animated 'Wee Man' in December 1997. The commercials featured the 'Wee Man' cartoon character in humorous situations, one with his head being pounded by a hammer. Askit is then administered for the alleviation of this ailment with the tagline 'Ask for Askit'.

The company was bought by Roche before being taken over by German pharmaceutical giant Bayer in 2006. In 2012 Bayer announced that it was withdrawing Askit from shelves.

Information and illustrations courtesy of Askit Laboratories

DID YOU KNOW?

In the 1950s in Canada, to meet the demands of Scots exiles there, Askit powders were made available for sale; in Toronto alone, thousands of Askit powders were sold every month.

Askit powders also found their way to Europe, Africa, Malaya, New Zealand and Australia, to name just a few places.

Within days of the news that Askit was being withdrawn from the shelves, the powders, which retailed at £2.44, were being sold on eBay for £249.99 a packet.

34

British Caledonian 🛡 *Airways*

The founder of British Caledonian Airways,
Adam Thomson, was the son of a shunter
on the London Midland & Scottish Railway.
He was educated at Rutherglen Academy,
Coatbridge College and the Royal Technical
College, now Strathclyde University.

In 1944, when he was seventeen, he joined the Fleet Air Arm and was sent to Canada for pilot training. By the time he was demobbed, he was a qualified pilot with aspirations to start his own airline. He therefore obtained a commercial pilot's licence, and two years after the war he and a partner acquired a Walrus biplane to fly mail to the fishing fleets and to give joyrides to holidaymakers at Largs on the River Clyde. While Thomson said it was a lot of fun, he could not get financial backing to keep Amphibian Air Haulage, as his company was called, going.

After Amphibian folded, Thomson had a number of jobs – as a pilot instructor with the Ministry of Civil Aviation, flying biplanes from the Isle of Wight to the Channel Islands for Newman Airways, working commercially with British European Airways and West African Airways, and transporting troops around Africa and to Singapore for the Britavia airline.

After seventeen years of working for other people, Thomson felt it was time to have another go at fulfilling his ambition – to have his own airline. Help in that quarter came from John de la Haye, who worked for

Cunard Eagle Airways and was also planning to start his own airline as he thought the North Atlantic charter market was wide open for development.

Joining forces, the two men announced the formation of Caledonian Airways (Prestwick) Ltd at a press conference in Glasgow in April 1961. That was the easy part, finding the finance was not.

Numerous meetings that Thomson and his close associates, Bill Williams and Curly Walter, had with Scottish and English financiers were fruitless, as no one wanted to lend money to eager young men who wanted to start up an airline with insufficient money, no air service licences and no real experience of running a company. Travel agents also expressed disbelief, except Murray Vidockler who beavered away among Scottish organisations in the USA and raised vital resources.

Advertisement for British Caledonian Airways' flights to Nigeria.

There was a snag there, however, as the Air Licensing Board refused to allow more than 20 per cent American involvement and even then in non-voting shares only.

Undaunted, Thomson took out a second mortgage on his house, cashed in his insurance policies and cleaned out his bank account.

Travelling the length and breadth of Scotland, he took the hat round friends, and friends of friends, until eventually sufficient funds were raised to charter a DC-7C on a pay-as-you-fly basis from the Belgian airline Sabena. The plane was named the *Star o' Rabbie Burns*.

After months of relentless toil, the first Caledonian Airways' flight took place on 29 November 1961, St Andrew's Day – a charter carrying immigrants from Barbados. Other flights followed, and over Christmas 1961 the first transatlantic charter, Prestwick to New York, was operated under a US regulation that permitted sporadic flights.

Then came disaster. By the beginning of 1962 cash-flow problems were immense and in March the company's only aircraft crashed in Africa, killing 100 people. Although the result of the inquiry was mechanical failure beyond pilot control, a principal shareholder withdrew and the travel trade lost confidence. Caledonian carried on, however, and in April leased a second aircraft from Sabena, which went into service immediately as *Flagship Bonnie Scotland*, which by June was being used on average thirteen hours a day.

As the state-backed airlines controlled scheduled routes and fares (the 'International Goliath Airways' as Thomson called them), Caledonian's only way of growth was to offer low-fare charters and package holiday flights from Gatwick and Prestwick. It therefore specialised in transatlantic deals for 'affinity groups' with names such as 'Ma Brown's Paisley Buddies'. It also flew pilgrims to Mecca and migrants to Australia.

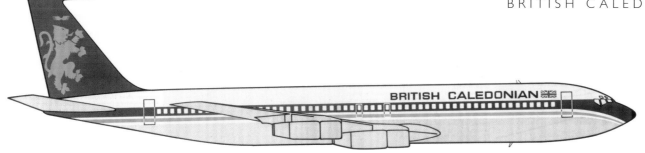

This drawing shows British Caledonian colours on a Boeing 707 used by the airline on all its intercontinental services and long-distance charters. The tail design represented the lion rampant of Scotland.

Caledonian survived into the jet age, and by 1968 it was running Boeing 707s to New York, Los Angeles and Singapore.

Meanwhile, as a response to consumer pressure for cheaper flights, the government-appointed Edwards Committee recommended that British European Airways and British Overseas Airways (merged in 1971 as British Airways) would benefit from competition from a 'second-force' airline such as Caledonian. On the strength of this, Thomson raised more capital and acquired the ailing British United Airways.

Based at Gatwick, Thomson's company was re-launched as British Caledonian on St Andrews Day 1970 and acquired routes to South America, West Africa, Europe, within Britain and later to the USA. Despite the Edwards Committee's conclusions, however, conditions remained difficult for small operators. British Caledonian (B Cal, as it was popularly known) could not compete with British Airways (BA). It was never able to increase its routes to much more than a tenth of BA's network. Furthermore, the collapse of the package holiday market after the 1973–74 oil crisis brought B Cal to its knees, with planes grounded and staff laid off.

Nevertheless, as it had done in its early days, B Cal survived and by 1975 was operating over 450 flights a week to twenty-three countries.

By the 1980s B Cal was the second largest airline in Britain and the ninth largest in Europe, with a fleet of twenty-seven jets servicing almost fifty international destinations. Travel writers had voted it the best airline in the world. It had moved from the long-haul charter business to scheduled flights. It provided more than half the traffic at Gatwick and had acquired new routes to Hong Kong, New York and Los Angeles. It had also introduced a £99 return fare to New York.

While it might have been expected that an entrepreneur such as Thomson would fare well under the Thatcher government, in the event he did not. The government wished to privatise British Airways, and Thomson suffered a big blow in 1983 when ministers rejected a proposal by him for the transfer of a significant part of BA routes to B Cal in case it damaged BA's flotation prospects. After losing that fight, B Cal suffered other blows. Because of the Falklands War, it lost its Buenos Aires route. It lost Tripoli because of tensions with Libya, and fear of terrorism cut demand on North Atlantic routes. Economic chaos in Nigeria hit its Lagos service and, ultimately, in 1987, its lucrative helicopter service between Heathrow and Gatwick was halted on environmental grounds.

Meanwhile, having been floated on the Stock Exchange, BA was going from strength to strength and decided to end competition from B Cal by making a £235 million takeover bid for it. Although Thomson responded to the bid by inviting Scandinavian Airlines System to become a major shareholder in B Cal, an increased bid by BA won the day, and in 1988 the two airlines were merged, making the aviation world a duller place without British Caledonian's tartan livery.

A 1920s' advertisement for 'Mother! Here comes the Castlebank man'.

Cover for Bowie's house magazine of January 1949, which showed a cute Mabel Lucie Atwell cartoon character. BASL stood for Bowie's Associated Services Ltd, the registered company's working name.

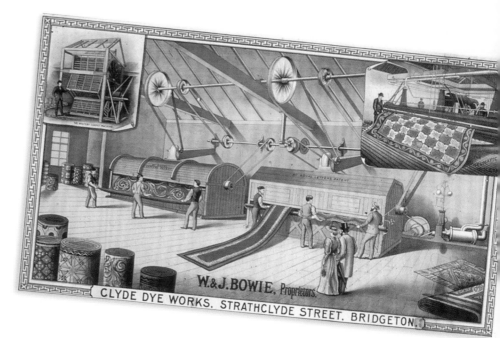

35

W & J Bowie's patent steam-powered carpet-beating machine.

Although, from Inverness to Penzance, Klick Photopoint and William Munro signs were familiar in almost every high street, most people had no inkling that Klick and Munro's origins lay in two rival laundry businesses in Glasgow in the second half of the nineteenth century.

The rival businesses were those of the Bowie and Kennedy families whose descendants own the Bowie Castlebank Group, the owners of Klick and Munro.

While the Bowie family's connection with laundry began with widow Annie Bowie going around factories with a wheelbarrow, offering to collect clothes for cleaning, it was her sons, William and John Bowie, who started a dyeing and scouring business some time between 1860 and 1861 in the east end of Glasgow. In 1870 the works moved to Strathclyde Street, Dalmarnock, creating the Clyde Dye Works. By 1879 there were thirteen branches and a new department, the Feather Room, where the dressing, curling and dyeing of feathers and feather boas was carried out.

In 1882, William and John Bowie built and patented a steam-powered carpet-beating machine that was so successful that there was a demand for it not only in Britain but also on the continent and even in America.

While carpet cleaning became the emphasis of Bowie's business, the dyeing department was kept busy. There was a year-round demand for clothing to be dyed black for mourning, and for faded garments to be dyed.

During the First World War, the company found it difficult to keep going. As cleaning and dyeing was not considered an essential industry, there was a shortage of chemicals and dyestuffs. After the war, the company leaned more and more towards garment-cleaning.

Although, in 1952, Bowie had opened its first unit branch (cleaning done on the premises) at 202 Byres Road, Glasgow, business was difficult as local entrepreneurs were eroding the traditional receiving-shop trade with their own on-site dry-cleaning. So in 1962 Bowie joined forces with a rival company, A. Kennedy & Sons Ltd of Anniesland, who owned the Castlebank Laundry. This created Bowie Castlebank – for both companies it had been either amalgamation or liquidation.

Now that the W & J Bowie story has been told, it is time to tell that of the company with which it amalgamated, A. Kennedy & Sons Ltd, which began with Alexander Kennedy opening a furniture business at 404 Byres Road, Glasgow, some time around 1870. However, he also cleaned carpets and the heavy household furnishings and draperies so fashionable in Victorian days. The cleaning side of the business prospered, and on 7 August 1878 a factory was opened in Castlebank Street.

In 1898, Castlebank inaugurated motor deliveries direct to their customers, and at the same time the first Castlebank branch office was opened in Glasgow,

the forerunner of the sunshine shops which, with their fresh yellow curtains, were to be seen all over Glasgow and the west of Scotland.

Meanwhile, there came news that a French genius, M. Louis Barbe of Lyons, France, had created a unique process of dry-cleaning under absolute seal, without even the friction of air. Introduced into Scotland by Castlebank in 1908, the Franco-Barbe process, as it was called, was exclusively Castlebank's.

After the Second World War, life at Castlebank more or less mirrored that at W & J Bowie until by 1962 neither had an option but to join forces with its rival, neither company being able to compete with the introduction of home washing machines.

By the late 1960s Bowie Castlebank acquired the Ayrshire-based Munro Cleaners, under which name the company began trading.

In 1981, the company was forced to diversify due to a decline in trade and bought a small photo-processing laboratory in Wishaw, which came along with the name 'Klick' on three shops in England. The move, however, seemed doomed when just a few months later a major client pulled out, taking a third of the business in the process. In desperation, Bowie Castlebank decided to offer a developing and printing service through its own dry-cleaning shops, and from then on there was no looking back for Klick Photopoint, as this side of the business became known as.

In December 2008, the Bowie Castlebank Group went into administration. The photo-processing business had been hit by the advance of digital photography, and the reduced number of clothes needing to be dry-cleaned had led to a contraction of the cleaning business.

Information and illustrations courtesy of the Bowie Castlebank Group

36

Stoddard CARPETS®

Stoddard was Scotland's largest and oldest carpet manufacturer and an international name.

Lion and Lioness. These picture carpets had a great vogue in the Middle East where they were in demand as part of a marriageable girl's dowry. They were not used as floor coverings but were prized as wall hangings.

The company held the Royal Warrant, and over the years carpeted royal palaces, embassies, stately homes, luxury passenger liners, exclusive hotels and thousands of homes worldwide.

The founder of the company, American Arthur Francis Stoddard, an autocrat with a domineering temperament and a strong sense of social justice, was born in 1810 into a well-connected and wealthy family of British descent who had settled in Massachusetts in 1639. Stoddard began his working life with his uncle, Arthur Tappan, a silk merchant and importer of dry goods in New York. Within a short time, he became a partner in the firm of Peter Denny, Importers, New York and was employed as its London representative, giving him the opportunity to travel both to Britain and to continental Europe.

Because of a slump in the United States that ruined his uncle's importing business, Stoddard left America

in 1844, intending to set himself up in London as an agent catering to Americans and Europeans wishing to buy British goods. Stoddard never made it to London. He docked at Greenock and made for Glasgow where he set up as a commission agent at Princes Square, 48 Buchanan Street.

Whatever the reason for his change of destination, it was a lucky one, as A. & S. Henry, merchants and commission agents, Manchester, who were looking for a Glasgow outlet, appointed him their Glasgow partner. They made a wise choice, for the company soon had branches in Dundee, Belfast, Bradford and Huddersfield.

While Stoddard decided to live in Britain rather than America, thousands of people were doing the reverse – leaving Britain in search of prosperity and freedom in America. The nineteenth century had been beset by economic and political crises, and by 1852 Paisley's main industries, shawl manufacturing and silk weaving,

A drawing of Arthur Francis Stoddard derived from descriptions of him.

One of Stoddard's earliest tapestry carpets, woven in 1864.

During the difficult times, Stoddard also found business slow as the American Civil War had brought with it a steady increase in duties. He therefore decided to end his association with A. & S. Henry rather than suffer huge losses, and in 1862 he resigned from the partnership and retired from business.

Stoddard's retirement did not last long for within months he had bought Patrickbank textile mill in Elderslie, which had just closed down. Why Stoddard bought the business that was to be the foundation of the Stoddard carpet empire was vague, even to his son, Frederick, who wrote: 'What the inducements were to purchase is not clear as he knew nothing of the business.' Maybe he was bored with retirement and wanted the interest and challenge of a new venture? Whatever the reason, Stoddard set about developing his company, which he named the Glenpatrick Carpet Mills.

The original weaving shed held twenty-four people, but numbers rose quickly. Stoddard, with his business experience and connections as well as his wealth, succeeded where others had failed. Within five years, he was selling three-quarters of the company's production in the United States, and when hostile American tariffs forced him to look for new markets, he found them in Europe.

When Stoddard died in 1882, Charles Bine Renshaw, his son-in-law, became sole partner and in 1891 brought his brother, Arthur, into the business. Under the vigorous new management, the company expanded. New markets were found at home and abroad, and another factory was acquired, at Foxbar. In 1894 the firm was turned into a limited liability company with a capital of £350,000 – a large sum for a family business.

When Sir Charles Renshaw (as he had become) died in 1918, his brother, Arthur, became chairman. He, however, died a few months later.

had collapsed, killed by the cheaper materials woven on the new power Jaquard looms. The weavers and their families were starving, and charitable organisations chartered ships to take them to America for what they hoped would be a better life.

One of Sir Charles's last actions in 1918 was to bring the Caledonian Carpet Company of Stirling and Ronald, Jack and Company of Paisley into the Stoddard fold by an exchange of shares. The amalgamation with Ronald, Jack and Company had links with the past – it was the Ronalds' mill that Stoddard had bought in 1862, W. H. Ronald had become a director of Stoddard and Stuart Jack, part-owner and managing director of Ronald, Jack and Company, was the son of Peter Jack junior, who had helped the Ronalds make a fresh start more than fifty years before.

Under the chairmanship of Sir Stephen Renshaw, son of Sir Charles, Stuart Jack and David Yellowlees successfully steered the group through the difficult days of the Depression of the 1930s and the Second World War, during which carpet-making was stopped.

When the Elderslie factory was reopened for carpet manufacturing in 1946, Stoddard began its greatest period of expansion under the chairmanship of Robert A. Maclean (later Sir Robert), who had joined the company in 1946 having before the war been a partner in James Templeton, the Glasgow carpet manufacturer. The expansion began in 1947 with the purchase of Douglas Reyburn, Kilmarnock, a woollen spinning mill. This was to safeguard raw material supplies. Henry Widnell and Stewart of Midlothian became part of the Stoddard group in 1959.

In 198, Stoddard Holdings acquired Templeton Carpets and Kingsmead Carpets. Rationalisation followed, with the closure of the Henry Widnell and Stewart manufacturing plant and then the huge Templeton manufacturing facilities. Kingsmead Carpets were sold in 1986. In 1988, Stoddard Holdings and Sekers International merged to form Stoddard Sekers International PLC. BMK was acquired in 1991.

In 2002, manufacturing at Elderslie ceased. This was because of a reduction in demand for traditional Axminster carpets as consumer preferences had moved towards less patterned and cheaper tufted products. A downsized Axminster operation was relocated to the company's Riverside plant in Kilmarnock.

Despite having a unique blend of high-quality design, traditional craftsmanship and the most advanced manufacturing technology, by the beginning of January 2005, mounting losses led to the company calling in the receivers. However, over-capacity in the UK carpet manufacturing section and overseas competition prevented a survival plan being put in place. Less than two months later the company ceased trading, and another of Scotland's great companies was no more.

Information and illustrations courtesy of Stoddard

Westminster Abbey with the Stoddard carpet laid ready for the royal wedding in 1947. Walter J. Bartram, the company's chief designer, painted the scene.

Templeton

The Twelve Apostles Carpet laid out in the Stoddard car park in November 2003. The photograph shows just how large the carpet is when compared with the size of the cars around it.

While the present generation might not be aware of the name 'Templeton' in relation to carpets, previous ones have no difficulty in recognising it, for James Templeton & Co. was once the largest and most important carpet firm in the world.

It was founded on the manufacture of chenille carpets, renowned for their softness, richness and beauty. To have one of these carpets was a status symbol, and people would speak with pride of their Templeton carpet.

The Templeton story started around 1820 when James Templeton, a farmer's son from Campbeltown, left home to work in Mr Rose's wholesale drapery business in Glasgow. Because of a decline in the drapery trade, however, he moved to Liverpool in 1823 and through a firm there obtained a lucrative post in Mexico. He was twenty-one years old when he left for Mexico, and when he returned to Britain three years later, he had savings of around £1,000 with which he intended starting his own business. Meanwhile, while looking around for the right opportunity, he began working for a Glasgow gingham manufacturer, and it was not until 1829 that he set up as a shawl manufacturer in Paisley, the Mecca of the world's shawl-making industry. No lady of fashion could be without a Paisley shawl.

Their texture was the finest, their designs intricate and beautiful.

In Paisley, Irish weaver, William Quiglay, had been making shawls from round chenille, a velvety fabric originating in France and highly popular for curtains and table covers. Around 1837, while experimenting, he discovered that by steaming and pressing he was able to keep all the chenille tufts on one side, making them take the shape of a 'V' with the cotton warps at the base.

Quiglay showed his findings to James Templeton, who was astounded. Where round chenille was coarse, irregular and gave a fuzzy design, the new material was fine, smooth and gave a clear design. Not being reversible, however, it was unsuitable for shawls or curtains, and Quiglay had no idea what it could be used for. James Templeton, however, knew exactly what it was perfect for – carpets, where only one side was visible in use. By adding a solid backing to give weight and strength to the chenille, which on its own was a beautiful but flimsy piece of cloth, rich velvety carpets of any size and colouring could be produced more quickly and cheaply than traditional hand-woven Axminsters.

Templeton and Quiglay produced a sample rug that more than lived up to expectations, motivating them to apply for a patent. In 1839, with Templeton paying all the expenses, this was granted in the names of Quiglay and Templeton and gave protection for fourteen years.

James Quiglay, however, although an expert weaver was a simple man, and no sooner was the patent granted than he announced that he did not want to be a partner. He therefore allowed James Templeton to retain the patent's sole rights in exchange for a lump sum plus a guarantee of employment when manufacturing began. Six months later, Quiglay sailed for America and was never heard of again.

James Templeton went on to set up a factory in King Street, Calton (now Redan Street), and started the first-ever manufacture of chenille carpets. When this factory burned down on Christmas Day 1856, he found new premises in William Street (now Templeton Street), and that was the beginning of what became the world's most famous carpet factory.

In 1888, Templeton acquired the patent for a spool Axminster loom, a development of the Skinner loom in America. Thirty looms were ordered and the famous Albert Mill facing Glasgow Green was built to house them. Started in 1889 and modelled on the Doge's Palace in Venice, it is one of Glasgow's most exotic buildings and is such an architectural landmark that it featured on a stamp when Glasgow was the European City of Culture in 1990.

The demise of Templeton started when it bought Grays of Ayr in July 1969. This put such a financial strain on Templeton that a couple of months later it accepted an offer from the Guthrie Corporation, a rubber and palm oil organisation that wanted to buy into the carpet industry. Unfortunately, Guthrie, trading under the name of British Carpets, was not knowledgeable about carpet manufacturing and that, coupled with a downturn in the industry, meant that Templeton did not make a profit, and in 1981 it was taken over by Stoddard Carpets, which closed its manufacturing facilities.

While Templeton's carpet factory might have ceased production, people still talk about Templeton carpets, as the name was a byword for quality. In fact, such was the quality of the carpets that many people still have them in their homes looking almost as good as new.

Illustrations courtesy of Stoddard Carpets